CLOSERTOGETHER, FURTHERAPART

THE EFFECT OF TECHNOLOGY AND THE INTERNET

ON PARENTING, WORK, AND RELATIONSHIPS

CLOSER TOGETHER, FURTHER APART

THE EFFECT OF TECHNOLOGY AND THE INTERNET ON PARENTING, WORK, AND RELATIONSHIPS

ROBERT WEISS, LCSW, CSAT-S

JENNIFER P. SCHNEIDER, MD, PhD

Gentle Path
PRESS

Gentle Path Press
P.O. Box 3172
Carefree, Arizona 85377
gentlepath.com

Copyright © 2014 by Gentle Path Press

All rights reserved. No part of this publication may be used or reproduced,
stored or entered into a retrieval system, transmitted, photocopied,
recorded, or otherwise reproduced in any form by any mechanical or
electronic means, without the prior written permission of the author, and
Gentle Path Press, except for brief quotations used in articles and reviews.

First edition: 2014

For more information regarding our publications,
please contact Gentle Path Press at 1-800-708-1796 (toll-free U.S. only)

ISBN: 978-0-9850633-3-7

Editor's note: All the stories in this book are based on actual
experiences. The names and details have been changed to protect the
privacy of the people involved. In some cases, composites have been created.

DOWN TO YOU
Words and Music by JONI MITCHELL
© 1973 (Renewed) CRAZY CROW MUSIC.
All Rights Administered by SONY/ATV MUSIC PUBLISHING,
8 Music Square West, Nashville, TN 37203.
All Rights Reserved

I've come up with a set of rules that describe our reactions to technologies.

1. *Anything that is in the world when you're born is normal and ordinary and is just a natural part of the way the world works.*
2. *Anything that's invented between when you're fifteen and thirty-five is new and exciting and revolutionary and you can probably get a career in it.*
3. *Anything invented after you're thirty-five is against the natural order of things.*

—Douglas Adams, author of The Hitchhiker's Guide to the Galaxy

CONTENTS

< ix >

PREFACE

The original intent of writing *Closer Together, Further Apart* was to explore the problems that digital technology appeared to be having on our relationships, especially our intimate ones. We were motivated to write this based on the outpouring of media reports on how technology is *overrunning and ruining* Western culture, along with "cocktail party conversations" where we heard much of the same. Curiously, as our research deepened our book premise quickly morphed into a much broader and more balanced analysis of the effects of digital technology on our daily lives.

We made some unanticipated discoveries along the way, and we expect that you will too. Here are just a few things we learned:

- Digital devices of today are just another part of the human/technological evolution—much like the invention of the wheel, printing press, the light bulb, and the splitting of atoms.
- Today's generation gap is different than any other generation gap we've seen because generations are not having conversations in the same way. Much of modern culture is embroiled in a profound, yet mostly unseen generation gap. The digital world has shifted how we communicate and share opinions. People of all ages are often literally separated by the very tools they use to communicate. Younger people live in a more digital and social media based environment while older adults increasingly report feeling left behind.

< xi >

- The escalation of addictive behaviors has been and always will be driven by technological advances. Most people are able to appreciate more immediate, escalated pleasures that technology provides us. A small sector of the population, typically the most emotionally vulnerable, will end up addicted.
- Humans are readily adaptable to change. That being said, some tend to adapt better or faster than others; those others will struggle and may even choose to ignore or rebel against change. When people don't have the courage to change, the result could be that they are left out of the relationships that they care about the most.
- The brains of our children are now evolving in sync with digital technology. Their brains have changed because of the electronic devices we have been placing into their hands at increasingly earlier stages of their development. The generation growing up now will differ from their parents more completely than any previous generation.

Our hope is that this book will be an eye opener, especially for skeptics who view the Internet, digital technology, and the rise of social media as signs pointing toward the inevitable decline of humanity and our culture. We believe *Closer Together, Further Apart* will be a great place for people from different generations to begin a nuanced, meaningful conversation that can help close that growing "generation gap." To help with this, we created a *Reading Group Guide* on page 203 to get that conversation started. A glossary of terms, beginning on page 181, is also available to get you up to speed on the latest tech terminology.

As you read this book, we invite you to personally explore how your relationships with others and with your sense of time, priority, and place have changed as a result of digital technology. Technology changes so rapidly that it's hard to keep up. We'll start out by looking at where it all began.

< xii >

ACKNOWLEDGMENTS

A giant shout out to Scott Brassart, our co-editor and research guide. Without Scott this book would not have been written—period. Scott, you are an amazing, good man. To Corrine Casanova of Gentle Path Press, a woman we've both known for nearly 20 years, thank you for being a superb editor and a quiet visionary behind the scenes. Thank you for all you do for us and so many others to get the work and word out there!

Rob Weiss

Kudos go out to my husband, Jonathan Westerman, if only because living with an author by definition, means being a patient, loving and creative man. Jon, you are all that and more. I have also been both shoved and supported into embracing the world and media of the 21st century by dear friends and colleagues like Rebekah Iliff and Kristen Tischhauser at AirPR and talkTECH, Dr. Stefanie Carnes, Dr. Patrick Carnes, Tami VerHelst at the International Institute for Trauma and Addiction Professionals and Brené Brown whose quiet vision is reshaping our world.

Further shout outs to Charlie Risien and Debra Kaplan along with Dr. David Sack, Keith Arnold, Vera Appleyard, and Lori Shannon at Elements Behavioral Health. Thanks too to my dear friend and reader, Eve Niedergang, you are amazing! Thanks also to Laura Maxey, Diana Lombardi, and Annette Banca of the 5WPR team for embracing this book and all that it represents. And to Steve Jobs, whose visionary, integrative thinking changed all of our lives and rocked the world that we thought we knew.

< xiii >

Finally, thank you to the hundreds of people who have taken the time to share their views with me during conferences, online, and events all over the world. Each of you has offered some gem or viewpoint along the way that has shaped the meaning of the world described in *Closer Together, Further Apart*.

Jennifer Schneider

I would like to acknowledge the support of Marni Dittmar, Lucia Yao, and David Sims, librarians at the Tucson Medical Center Library. Without their willingness to send me dozens of references on short notice, I could not possibly have accomplished the research and writing that I contributed to this book! I would also like to thank my late daughter Jessica Grace Wing, a big participant in the early days of the Internet revolution and one of the first volunteer "digital natives." I wish she could have lived to see how the Internet has changed the world. Last but not least, I would like to thank my son, Ben Wing, whose knowledgeable and thoughtful critique of this book resulted in some valuable changes.

< xiv >

INTRODUCTION

The Historical Impact of Technology on Human Relationships and Communication

The date that divides human history into two equal parts is well within living memory. The world of today is as different from the world I was born in as that world was from Julius Caesar's. I was born in the middle of human history, to date, roughly. Almost as much has happened since I was born as happened before.
—Kenneth Boulding, economist (1910–1993)

Throughout most of human history, the ways in which people communicated and interacted remained relatively constant, especially over the course of any single generation. The only real communication changes from the dawn of time until the mid to late nineteenth century occurred with the advent of language, the written word, and the arrival of wired communication via the telegraph.

In the past, most people became better at meeting and mating as they matured, thanks to the wisdom of experience. However, over the course of one's lifetime back then the basics of human interaction remained roughly unchanged—relationships began and developed through introduction, face-to-face interpersonal interaction, and the occasional letter. We met, talked, batted eyelashes, gossiped, broke bread, coupled up, sometimes had sex, and sometimes killed each other. Occasionally some of us skipped the earlier tasks and went straight to the coupling, sex, or killing, but the general idea—that our relationship with other human beings was, until very recently, almost wholly dependent on our proximity to them—remained intact. We have always needed to be in the

< 1 >

same physical space at the same time to interact. But in recent years the meaning of "proximity" and "being in the same place at the same time" has changed dramatically. Telecommunication—telegrams, telephones, radio, television, and, more recently, the Internet, smartphones, tablets, and other forms of digital technology—has turned the entire planet into one giant room where anyone and everyone with Internet access can easily and instantly connect and interact.

From Prehistory to the Start of Modern Times

For most of human existence, people lived in small, widely dispersed, often nomadic groups of usually no more than a few hundred to a few thousand members. Somebody could live an entire lifetime without encountering even one member of another tribe or clan. Typically, then, our opportunities for socializing were limited to the particular group (community) into which we were born. Intimacy involved meeting (or more likely being set up to meet), mating, and sharing goods with the boy or girl next door. We got to know that person through a series of interactions, fell in love (or not), had sex, likely reproduced, grew old, and died.

Prior to the advent of language—somewhere around 200,000 years ago, give or take a few centuries—humans relied on drums, clapping, gestures, fire, smoke, whistles, horns, and various grunts, primal screams, and moans to interact, communicate, and share important information. This rich history helps explain why shared popular songs, dance, and rhythm remain ingrained in our culture. Research tells us that even today the most primitive parts of our brains (even while in a comatose or unconscious state) will deeply and instinctually become activated in response to the rhythms, drumbeats, and baselines of popular music.[1] The tribal sounds that we now hear blaring from our home and car audio systems not only keep our fingers tapping but also hold the same power to bring humans together as did the claps and drumbeats of our ancestors.

However, these ancient methods of communication were not without their shortcomings. Claps, whistles, gestures, grunts, horns, and howls could be heard or seen only by those who were nearby. The ef-

< 2 >

fort needed to reach large numbers of people, to communicate between friendly or rival tribes, for instance, was enormous. Either a runner needed to be dispatched, often traversing dangerous terrain to deliver a message, or large bonfires needed to be lit—no easy task at the time—so that smoke signals could be sent. Furthermore, the meanings of these communications were open to misinterpretation. For instance, it was likely difficult to know if the distant blowing of a horn signaled victory, religious sacrifice, or imminent danger; if drumbeats were a warning or an invitation; whether a primal scream meant "Go away!" or "Look out, there's a hungry tiger over that next hill!" Nevertheless, these communication methods were at least moderately effective, as evidenced by the fact that we still use them today. We still clap our hands to get someone's attention or express appreciation, honk a car horn to say "Get out of the way," or moan from deep within ourselves as expressions of both pleasure and grief.

The development of spoken language—our ability to form words and then sentences conveying specific, even nuanced information—represented a giant leap forward in the evolution of human relations. Rather than a male simply pointing to a fertile woman's genitals and then pushing her down into the dirt for sex, he could speak to her, saying something like, "I find you very attractive and arousing. With your permission, I'd very much like to make love to you, or at least buy you some dinner." This, all in all, feels like a much more pleasant encounter for everyone involved.

After the dawn of mutually understood gesture and spoken language, for many generations the only technological advance in human interpersonal relations was the refinement of those languages and the beginnings of our ability to write them down. Only when the wheel came along in roughly 4000 BC did we take another leap forward. The wheel, particularly when combined with the horse-drawn chariot (in about 2000 BC), enabled people to travel from place to place more easily. In that moment, the wheel changed our experience of "proximity." It was now easier to actually meet up with someone. Because of this technology, more people interacted, more ideas were exchanged, trade increased, and various tribal languages began morphing into common,

< 3 >

widely used languages. As transportation advances encouraged increased trade over longer distances, more and more people were forced to learn other languages and customs. This was the early beginning of multicultural exchange. Simply put, as humankind developed technologies useful to a more productive existence, these technologies influenced how we communicate and develop relationships, even to this day.

However, it was the invention of spoken language and, later, written communication that was the technological leap with the most profound effect on human interaction. Writing, in particular, has had a lasting impact as the written word is both transportable and preservable. With the advent of the written word, the thoughts, past experiences, and ideas of individuals and whole cultures could be chronicled and shared with people in other places. Indeed, writing allowed us to both send and receive information from people living too far away to readily visit, also allowing us to convey our history, knowledge, and existence to future generations. No longer did we have to depend on song or storytelling to pass down this vital information. Furthermore, we could now turn to recorded history to (hopefully) learn from our ancestors' survival successes and failures.

In ancient times, the abilities to both travel and write were privileges of the elite. Horse-drawn chariots and other means of "rapid transit" were beyond the economic reach of the masses, and education was a luxury few could afford, even in the rare cities and towns in which it was available. Even wealthier, educated people sometimes had difficulty obtaining the quills, ink, and paper needed for writing, as these items were scarce. Consequently, up until a few hundred years ago the vast majority of humanity continued to solely communicate face-to-face, in the same room, using spoken language. Even the invention of the printing press in 1441 did little to change this, except among well-heeled denizens of the more technologically advanced nations. It wasn't until the 1800s that travel (think various applications of the steam engine) and the written word (driven by those with a fervent interest in spreading both religious and political dogma) became accessible to commoners—and even then this occurred only in wealthier nations.

< 4 >

The 800th Lifetime

In his seminal 1970 book *Future Shock*, Alvin Toffler wrote: "Almost invariably, research into the effects of change concentrate on the destinations toward which change carries us, rather than the speed of the journey. [But] the *rate* of change has implications quite apart from, and sometimes more important than, the *directions* of change."[2] In other words, human society is affected not only by changes, particularly technological changes, but by the speed with which they occur.

A useful concept to illustrate the ever-increasing pace of technological change is that of the 800th lifetime, introduced in *Future Shock*. There Toffler divided the approximately 50,000 years of relatively traceable human history into "lifetimes" of roughly 62 years, coming up with 800 lifetimes. He notes that the first 650 of those lifetimes were spent in caves. He then tells us that only during the last 70 lifetimes has it been possible to communicate effectively from one lifetime to the next (via written history), and only during the last six lifetimes has a significant percentage of the human population been able to access that written history/communication. He also notes that most of the products we now use on a day-to-day basis were invented very, very recently—during the 800th lifetime.[3] For purposes of this book, our focus is the products or technologies that relate to the ways in which humans currently communicate and interact. This means we're not particularly interested in washing machines. Except we are. Why? Because washing machines have, in their own way, affected interpersonal relationships.

Really?

Yes, really. Before Whirlpool and Tide came along, women took their small children and the family's dirty laundry down to the river so they could rinse the soiled garments and beat them against rocks to knock out the dirt. While there, the children played together and the mothers had a chance to socialize *face-to-face* with their peers. And this thousands-of-years-old venue for female and child socialization is completely gone today—all thanks to the washing machine. This does not mean that women and kids no longer socialize and communicate with one another. Obviously they do. They just do it in different ways and different places. Numerous other inventions—too many to list here—have simi-

< 5 >

larly changed how women, men, children, families, communities, and nations connect and communicate. This basic idea, that human-crafted technology impacts the nature of human communication, relationships, and thereby human evolution, is a main theme of this book.

What the Scholars and Philosophers Have to Say

Over the last 150 years, sociologists and anthropologists have created various theories on social and cultural evolution. Among these noted scholars is Lewis H. Morgan, a contemporary of Charles Darwin, who identified technological progress as the driving factor in the development of human civilization. Morgan divided humanity into three major stages—savagery, barbarism, and civilization—relying on *technological milestones* to separate one from the next. In the savage era we had fire, the bow and arrow, and pottery; in the barbarian era we developed agriculture, metalworking, and domesticated animals; in the civilized era we invented the alphabet.[4] In other words, for about 730 lifetimes humans were savages and barbarians, and then we learned to write.

Gerhard Lenski, a later philosopher, stated that the more information a society has, the more advanced it is. He viewed human development as occurring in four stages based on advances in the art/science of communication.

Lenski's Four Stages of Human Development

Stage One	Generational information was passed on via genetic material.
Stage Two	Humans gained the ability to perceive and develop wisdom, learning through experience and by watching the actions of others.
Stage Three	Humans developed logic and started using signs (or pictographs) to represent their experiences. (Example: cave drawings)
Stage Four	Humans developed language, abstract symbols, and writing.

< 6 >

Lenski's basic theory is that advances in the technology of communication translate into advances in the economic system, the political system, and virtually every other sphere of human existence.[5]

Both Morgan and Lenski identified the final sociological/anthropological leap based on the ability of human beings to communicate *beyond the face-to-face*, to interact without having to physically occupy the same space. And, as Toffler eloquently explains in *Future Shock*, that ability has been with us in a meaningful way for only a very brief period, really only picking up steam in the last two hundred years or so as the printed word became slowly but steadily more accessible.

The Great Leap

Metaphorically speaking, humans got up off of their hands and knees, brushed off the muck and mire, and started not so much walking as sprinting with the advent of *telecommunication*—the transmission of organized and understandable electric signals over long distances. Happily, telecommunications provide the specificity that smoke signals, drums, and horns lacked. A telegram, for instance, could say, "Meet me in St. Louis at the Atwater Hotel, noon July 21, to discuss the marriage of your daughter to my son. STOP." No mistaking the meaning of *that* communiqué.

The first useful telecommunications device, of course, was the telegraph, which Samuel Morse successfully tested in 1838. By late 1861 the first transcontinental telegraph system was established, and by the end of the nineteenth century telegraph cables connected every continent but Antarctica. Seemingly overnight, the transmission of information across great distances no longer relied on the vagaries of ships, carrier pigeons, and pony express riders. News, data, and other information could be transmitted almost instantaneously to virtually any major city. From there, it could be disseminated to others via the written and spoken word. In less than half a century the telegraph managed to connect virtually everyone on the planet.

In a relative flash, other telecommunications technologies arrived via telephone (1876), radio (1896), and television (1927).

< 7 >

Suddenly like magic, someone with the right expertise and devices could communicate with great masses of people all at the same time. Franklin Delano Roosevelt guided a struggling nation through the Great Depression with his inspirational "fireside talks" on the radio. Martin Luther King Jr. broadened the minds of not only the people directly in front of him, but millions of others who heard him on radio and saw him on television. Both of these men would rank highly on any list of "great leaders in history," not only for their intelligent ideas and personal charisma, but because they understood and capitalized on the power of mass communication.

Toffler wrote in *Future Shock* about this communications explosion: "In our lifetime the boundaries have burst. Today the network of social ties is so tightly woven that the consequences of contemporary events radiate instantaneously around the world. A war in Vietnam alters basic political alignments in Peking, Moscow, and Washington, touches off protests in Stockholm, affects financial transactions in Zurich, triggers secret diplomatic moves in Algiers."[6] Note that Toffler penned this statement in 1970, decades before the Internet! Amazingly, he was referencing the now seemingly archaic, limited, and slow news sources known as newspapers, radio, and television.

Kenneth Boulding (1910–1993), whose quote we use at the beginning of this chapter, witnessed the rise of the telephone, radio, and television, along with the automobile, the airplane, and rocket ships. One could argue that his comment, "Almost as much has happened since I was born as happened before," is quite the understatement.

Time it Took for New Communication Technologies to Enter the Homes of 50 million people (US)

Radio	38 years
Television	13 years
Internet	4 years
Social networking	16 months
Smartphone apps	9 months

< 8 >

From Analog to Digital: Where Everything Old is New Again

One tangible way to illuminate the past three decades of technological change is to note that as a society and a species we have shifted from an analog world to a digital one. In the analog world of the past, physical movement was necessary to perform a specific function. In today's digital world, most of our desired experiences require little physical movement beyond the occasional tap of an on-off button, a sweep of our finger, a spoken word or keyboard stroke. While this shift may seem obvious based on all the bleeping, vibrating, and multi-tasking going on, it can actually be difficult to identify in our day-to-day existence how profound these changes are. For example, let's consider the history of the car radio.

When the car radio was introduced in the 1930's (by Motorola, a company named and founded for just that purpose), the process of listening to the radio involved physically moving a series of knobs, bars and dials that controlled a large, heavy vacuum tube driven receiver and amplification device mounted into the dashboard of your automobile. To raise or lower the volume you physically turned a knob that magnified the sound level being produced. To find your favorite station, you had to turn another knob that would visibly move a bar across the AM frequency band. By moving the bar just so; you could *find your station*. To maintain good sound, the dial had to be frequently adjusted by hand as radio signals faded in and out as you drove from place to place. Careful listening was the key to successfully guiding the knob as you attempted to find and tune into the strongest signal source.

By the 1950's this technology had evolved to allow users to actually preset the car radio to their favorite stations rather than constantly having to turn a knob to locate them. This analog evolution allowed users to push one of a set of mechanically keyed buttons. The sheer force of your push would physically slide the bar along to your preselected broadcast frequency.

By the early 1960's as transistors quickly replaced vacuum tubes, car audio became more compact and efficient allowing for the addition of FM frequencies. The invention of stereo sound provided an even more varied experience. By the 1970's 8-track players became popular, fol-

< 9 >

lowed by the cassette tape. The 1980's brought our first taste of fully digitized music via compact discs (CDs), which though encoded in a digital format, were nonetheless "read" by mostly analog machines.

Now fully digital, in cars today we have available to us automatic signal-seeking radios that find the strongest signals for themselves often initiated by a vocal command, along with satellite transmitted music stations. These *radios* are now most often combined with plug-in digital music players (most commonly in the form of an Apple iPod). It may be worth noting too that the analog to digital evolution described here was more or less a seven decade process in the making. It did not happen overnight.

An interesting observation is that now, just like in 1935, you can still listen to the radio while driving. We just do it differently than they did over seven decades ago. While it is true that the digital revolution has brought a literal end to our purchase and ownership of previously popular analog devices such as telephones, cameras, printing presses, record players, rolodexes, and televisions, we still need, want and enjoy the experiences those products produced for us. We talk "on the phone," we still "take pictures," we "read books," and we continue to "listen to recorded music," and "watch TV." Most of these *experiences* are nearly the same as they were in days of yore, however, they are delivered in new ways.

While so much has changed that it may be difficult for someone to even grasp the relationship between a rolodex and the contacts icon on your cell phone, the function of both (analog and digital) devices remains the same. In 1960, no one would have known what the heck to do with a smartphone yet many of the functions our digital devices now provide (telephone, movies, books, maps, and cameras) would all have been quite familiar to them. It's just in a different format. Multiple generations have indeed shared similar experiences but in a profoundly dissimilar manner resulting in the "new generation gap" which is the focus of Chapter One.

There is no denying that we are in the midst of a tech-connect BOOM. Virtually everyone in the first and increasingly in the second world economies today owns or has access to a computer, smartphone,

< 10 >

or mobile device. Digital interaction has in less than three decades become an integral part of our worldwide daily routine. We check emails and texts, update our Facebook page, fire off a tweet or two, and then finish our morning coffee. This ever-increasing digital interconnectivity provides endless opportunities to support our very human needs for social interaction and feeling part of the larger community.

For partners, spouses, and families separated for long periods of time by work or military service, this tech-connect boom has been a godsend. Friends and family too distant for regular contact just a few years ago can now be intimately folded into each other's lives. Couples, children, and parents are able to bond long-distance in real time, sharing a growing child's latest milestone and even engaging in visual intimacy via webcams. Those not yet in a committed relationship can put technology to good use via e-dating, establishing and developing budding relationships with less focus than ever before on who lives where. We make friends, we share our experiences, we celebrate, and we commiserate via the Internet—one world, a growing, interactive community.

The digital world has also helped educate the general public about topics formerly considered too personal or embarrassing to discuss with friends and family or even a professional. Thanks to the Internet, nonjudgmental clinical information on mental illness, spousal abuse, sexuality, relationship intimacy, and drug and alcohol abuse can now be found online 24/7. This has helped to de-stigmatize formerly shameful topics and facilitate useful connections with like-minded individuals.

Perhaps the vast digital networks of like-minded individuals that form today via social media are merely a reflection of our deeply felt and unmet human need for a closer sense of community. Living in small family units is a fairly recent phenomenon. From pretty much the dawn of time up until the industrial revolution most men and women lived, ate, and shared their life experiences among large, closely knit communities. Most children were raised not by one set of parents, but rather an entire community.

In the past, people found both shelter and safety by living together. By doing so they were better protected from a seemingly unpredictable and dangerous world. While the past few hundred years of scientific

< 11 >

and technological advances have brought humanity vast new freedoms along with the relative safety to enjoy them, these advantages have also pushed us further and further apart. The now typical household of one or two adults living alone or with children would not have survived during those times. And though today we are able to both enjoy more mobility and are less dependent on friends and family for our physical survival, it may well be that our social needs have been profoundly ignored. In this vein, we wonder if the time that many of us now spend on social media hanging out with like-minded people, sharing our current status and connecting online with old friends, distant family and loved ones serves as a *good enough* digital replacement for the centuries of communal living that in modern life has for the most part eradicated.

Yakkety Yak, Don't Look Back

At the time of this writing, there are well over two billion Internet users worldwide. Asia leads the way with over one billion users and North America has more than 273 million—over three-quarters of our population. The least technologically developed continent, Africa, has just shy of 140 million users, which is only about 13 percent of that continent's population, but the number of African users has increased nearly 3,000 percent in the first twelve years of the twenty-first century. *Nearly one-third of the world's population is online.*[7] And that number increases every single moment. To call the Internet a ubiquitous worldwide phenomenon would be a vast understatement. Essentially, we live in a new "golden age" of information and communication. We are interconnected in ways that were undreamed of a mere decade ago. In technologically advanced nations today virtually anyone, no matter where he or she is, can immediately connect with almost any other person.

Digital technology—primarily the Internet but also cell phones, cable TV, and other innovations—has, in less than a single generation, dramatically and permanently altered the ways in which humans connect and communicate on our little green and blue planet. Conversations and information transfers that once either weren't possible or took days to complete now occur in an instant. Both the pace and breadth of human interactions have infinitely increased.

< 12 >

A Recap

Digital technology has also brought amazing advances into human interactivity and relationships. Today it is possible to be "virtually present" with someone on the other side of the planet, on an airplane, or even in outer space. We can "be together" with absolutely anyone, anywhere. Our actual location is rapidly becoming irrelevant. These technological advances are profoundly affecting humankind, forcing change on multiple levels. Throughout this book we will explore what these changes may or may not mean to humanity and our individual ability (and even our desire) to form and maintain meaningful interpersonal relationships both in the short- and long-term.

< 13 >

CHAPTER ONE

The New Generation Gap

Everything comes and goes
Marked by lovers and styles of clothes
Things that you held high
And told yourself were true
Lost or changing as the days come down to you
—Joni Mitchell, Down to You

Generally speaking, people born before 1980 are considered to be *digital immigrants*, and those born after 1980, *digital natives*.[1] Digital natives are people who grew up actively using and engaging with computers and the Internet, while digital immigrants did not. While this arbitrary 1980 dividing line is not a hard-and-fast rule, typically, digital natives unquestioningly appreciate and value the role that digital technology plays in their lives, whereas digital immigrants hold mixed views about how modern communications technology has impacted their lives. To better understand this concept, consider the following two situations.

Situation one: A group of friends are at a busy restaurant. Everyone at the table is under age twenty-eight (digital natives). Several people are chatting with each other in conversation, while others appear to be fully engaged with their digital communication devices—texting, tweeting, and dropping in on Facebook. Everyone looks relaxed. There seems to be no hurry or worry about who is available to talk or what others are doing. The group appears as a whole to understand that being digitally preoccupied, while also at dinner with friends, is acceptable, typical, and routine. The devices and people at the table have near equal status.

< 15 >

Situation two: A more age-differentiated group of people are sitting at a table at that same restaurant. About half of the people are forty-five or older (digital immigrants), while the rest of the group are younger professionals in their late twenties (digital natives). Several people are chatting with each other in active conversation, while others appear to be fully engaged with their digital communication devices. Unlike situation one, there is tension at this table. Several of the older diners are clearly annoyed with the younger adults. They look over at them impatiently, lips pursed, feet tapping under the table. Eventually one of the digital immigrants turns to the woman next to her and says, "When did a phone become more important than a human being?" Her same-age friend clucks and nods.

If these scenarios sound familiar, then you are getting a sense of the electronic media-based generational divide that is a strong theme throughout the book.

This rapidly widening separation between digital natives and digital immigrants has created a new generation gap. This gap has introduced conflicting methodologies and ideologies that ultimately affect nearly every facet of modern life. There are differences in the ways digital natives and digital immigrants conduct business and gather news and information, as well as how they both earn and spend their paychecks. Digital natives and digital immigrants can also differ significantly in the ways they define personal privacy, how they experience entertainment (music, books, and movies), even the ways they socially engage—including flirting, romancing, and having sex.

Scaling back to view the big picture, it becomes increasingly clear that in nearly every arena outside of face-to-face interactions, our basic forms of interpersonal communication and social connection have been utterly reformatted in a mere two to three decades. In some ways this sounds much like every other generation gap in history. However, previous generation gaps have mostly centered on younger people hearing and seeing the older generation but ultimately rejecting and/or devaluing their ideas and beliefs. *Today's generation gap is more about the younger generation being literally and figuratively separated from the older generation in many, if not most, aspects of their lives.* In other words, digital natives

< 16 >

often neither see nor hear their elders because, from a communications standpoint, digital immigrants and digital natives are literally "not in the same room."

Baby boomers will certainly remember the 1960s mantra "Don't trust anyone over thirty," first uttered by activist Jack Weinberg in relation to the Free Speech Movement. Today the mantra might be "Where are the people over thirty?" If you don't text, email, spend time on Twitter or Facebook, or blog, then you're not communicating or interacting with younger people. They simply don't know you exist.

Talkin' 'Bout My Generation ...

Beyond the obvious age differences, "generations" are typically defined by their use of slang; their choice of music and clothing; and their politics, social causes, and technological influences.

The "Digital Immigrant" Generations, Born 1901–1982

Generation	Dates Born
Greatest Generation	1901–1924
Silent Generation	1925–1945
Baby Boomer	1946–1964
Generation X	1965–1982

The *Greatest Generation* and the *Silent Generation* were the children and young adults of the Depression. They either fought in or supported the troops in World War II. These people experienced the advent of blues and jazz, listening to that music on newly evolving technologies like phonographs and radios. They were born into a world without television or microwave ovens. The formative moments in their lives were the *Titanic* disaster in 1912, Charles Lindbergh's transatlantic flight in 1927, the stock market crash of 1929, the Great Depression, and World Wars I and II. These were the first generations to ride in automobiles,

< 17 >

the first to have universal access to electricity and fully plumbed homes, and the first to be able to communicate in real time via telephone.

Those in the *Baby Boomer* generation were born during the post-WWII "baby boom." In their youth, they were typically associated with a rejection of the more traditional or "conservative" values of their parents. They are credited with generating both social upheaval and liberal change in the United States and throughout the Western world, resulting in a liberal versus conservative political and cultural divide that lives on to this day. Baby boomers listened to Elvis, the Beatles, and Motown on transistor radios and 45 rpm records. They grew up glued to television, enthralled by the *Ed Sullivan Show*, the *Brady Bunch*, *Gilligan's Island*, the *Twilight Zone*, and, of course, the *Wonderful World of Disney*. Early baby boomers (born 1946–1955) list the Cuban Missile Crisis; the assassinations of John F. Kennedy, Robert Kennedy, and Martin Luther King; the first moon landing; Roe versus Wade; the Vietnam war; Woodstock; and the civil rights, women's rights, and gay rights movements as formative events in their lives. Later boomers (born 1956–1964) were more conscious of Watergate, the Iran hostage crisis, raging inflation, gasoline shortages, and, of course, disco.[2]

Generation X (Gen X) includes people born between 1965 and 1982. They are often characterized as a "slacker" generation, though studies show their values and work ethic are not so different from those of their parents. This generation listened to pop, punk, alternative, rap, and hip hop music on their boom boxes and Sony Walkmans. Their lives were shaped by the 1973 oil crisis and subsequent years of worldwide financial recession, the 1986 Chernobyl disaster, the 1989 fall of the Berlin Wall, and the end of the Cold War. They played Donkey Kong and Mario Bros on increasingly sophisticated video gaming platforms. They experienced the earliest days of cable TV and were particularly influenced by *Sesame Street* and Music Television (MTV), the first network aimed specifically at them as a demographic. Gen Xers were also profoundly influenced by the AIDS epidemic, crack cocaine, and designer drug abuse. Some Gen Xers did not use personal computers and the Internet until early adulthood, while others had these technologies available to them earlier.

< 18 >

The "Digital Native" Generations, Born 1983 to Now

Generation	Dates Born
Generation Y	1983–2000
Generation Z	2001–present

Generation Y (Gen Y), also known as "Millennials," are more familiar with interactive communication, media, and digital technologies than prior generations. Gen Ys listen to hip hop, rap, indie (independent), post-grunge, electronic, techno, dubstep, R&B (rhythm and blues), rock, hardcore punk, metalcore, teen pop, pop punk, Eurodance, K-pop (Korean pop), C-pop (Chinese pop), J-pop (Japanese pop), Bhangra, and international music on iPods and other MP3 devices. They get their news online rather than reading a newspaper or watching the evening news. Gen Y is sometimes accused of suffering from "Peter Pan Syndrome," delaying rites of passage into adulthood (such as getting a job and moving out of the house).[3] Defining moments for Gen Ys include the tragedy of 9/11, the wars in Iraq and Afghanistan, the arrival of social media (Facebook and MySpace), the smartphone, the 2007–2008 global financial crisis, and the election of Barack Obama as United States president. *However, the single most defining characteristic of Gen Y is that its members use digital technology as a primary resource for communication, interaction, and information gathering.* They do so more often, more fluidly, and for far more purposes than previous generations.

Generation Z (Gen Z), also known as the "Always On" generation, *have never known a world without modern high-speed Internet.* Engaging with each other via social media is as natural to Gen Zs as breathing. They were born into a world of multitasking. The neurobiological, developmental, social, and educational impact of this way of living from birth onward is as yet unknown. In many ways, much like the baby boomers of yore, Gen Z is a true social experiment in the making because we really don't know what Gen Zs will look like in the future or how they will meet, work, or mate.

< 19 >

Here Today, Gone Tomorrow

A technology (or anything else) is obsolete when it is no longer used. Most often, obsolete means something is out of date and needs to be replaced by something newer and more efficient—or at least a bit shinier. Obsolete items are outmoded, outdated, archaic, antiquated, passé, and unfashionable. And nowhere does obsolescence arrive more quickly than in the world of communication technology.

Consider, for example, the telephone. Brent, a member of the Silent Generation, recalls that as a boy in upstate Washington he had to crank the phone to reach the operator. When Brent asked the operator to connect him with his friend Jimmy, the operator might say, "I think Jimmy is over at Bobby's house today. Let me check there," and more often than not she was right.

Brent's friend Scott, born on the cusp of the Baby Boomer and X Generations, used to dial his friend Michael's house when he wanted someone to play with. And if Michael wasn't home, so be it. Scott would have to call back later, leave a message with Michael's parents, or hop on his bicycle and pedal around the neighborhood to look for his friend.

Today when Scott's Gen Y nephew Matt wants to call his friend Marshall, he pulls his phone out of his pocket and simply says, "Call Marshall." The phone does as instructed, and no matter where Marshall is—he could be three states away, vacationing with his family—the call finds Marshall and he picks up. Matt has never spoken to a switchboard operator, never used a rotary dial, never used a pay phone, never called collect, never checked his answering machine, never been paged, and never paid for a long distance call. He has no need to remember a phone number and in fact he's never actually heard a phone "ring." The moniker "Ma Bell" means nothing to him. If he time traveled to Brent's childhood home in upstate Washington, he would have no idea that the strange wooden box hanging on the wall was a telephone. That's a mere nanobyte of how much technology has changed in just sixty years.

< 20 >

Obsolete or Rapidly Becoming Obsolete Communications/ Entertainment Technologies

- phonographs
- 8-tracks, cassettes, and reel-to-reel tapes
- transistor radios and boom boxes
- laser discs
- floppy discs
- analogue recordings and recording devices (tape)
- stereo receivers, tape decks, and turntables
- dictation machines
- Walkman and Discman personal stereos
- HAM and CB radios
- Super 8 and 16 mm film
- Betamax and VHS
- typewriters and carbon paper
- word processors
- dot-matrix printers
- dial-up modems
- land-based telephones
- watches (worn for functionality rather than as an accessory)
- PDAs and pagers
- print newspapers and printed phonebooks
- film cameras
- analog copy machines
- book and record collections
- photo albums

Some of these obsolete analog technologies will be missed, others not so much. For instance, no one laments the demise of screechy dial-up modems. Nor is anyone pining for the days of 8-track tapes (which would frequently stop in the middle of a song and switch tracks, interrupting the music). On the other hand, cassette tapes—the technology that replaced 8-tracks—are greatly missed by many Gen Xers because you could record onto a blank cassette tape, making a "mix tape" of your favorite songs. Giving a girl (or boy) a personalized mix tape was a great way to let her (or him) know how you felt, especially if that tape contained a liberal sprinkling of sappy love songs. Sure, with current technology you can e-share a personalized MP3 playlist, but it's

< 21 >

not the same as handing someone a cassette you've spent many hours constructing.

And let us not forget the physical places traditionally required to locate, interact with, and purchase the obsolete technologies that are disappearing from the American landscape.

Obsolete or Rapidly Becoming Obsolete Locations

- video and DVD rental stores
- music and record stores
- post offices*
- public libraries (as repositories for new books and periodicals)*
- newspaper stands
- mailboxes
- bookstores
- big box electronics stores
- telephone booths
- travel agencies

*While post offices and public libraries will likely continue in some social/community-based format, their original intended purpose and need has forever been altered and made increasingly irrelevant.

"Hand" Writing

It appears, too, that the skill-set of handwriting (the one that used to cause that permanent callus on your right or left middle finger) is also rapidly diminishing. Today, children from elementary school through college have a decreased need to communicate via any kind of handwritten document, particularly in cursive. According to a 2011 *New York Times* article, a university professor, on a whim, asked his undergrad students to raise their hands if they wrote anything in cursive as a way to communicate. None did.[4] In that article an elementary school principal says, "Schools today are preparing our kids for the 21st century. Is cursive really a 21st century skill?" For that matter, is writing anything by hand important? In response to that question, several students blogged the following thoughts:

< 22 >

- When kids get older, I guess they will have to use cursive to sign their names on documents, and that's good 'cause personally that's all I can write in cursive.
- I was done with cursive by 4th grade, so I can still read and write it, albeit slowly, but I see no practical use for this skill.
- A signature doesn't even need to be in cursive, technically. If the purpose is to provide identification by way of your own handwriting, now I can do that with a digital fingerprint.

Today in many high schools, teachers are forced to print *because the children being taught do not read cursive.* As we move away from "hand" writing, schools are now requiring proficiency in computer keyboarding by the time most students finish eighth grade. By 2015, all standardized American educational tests will be administered via computer. Cursive writing—in fact, any need for a pen or pencil—appears to be less and less relevant.[5]

Similar changes are occurring worldwide. A recent British survey, for example, found that on average most adults engage in actual handwriting (signatures aside) approximately once every forty-one days! One in three people surveyed said they had written nothing by hand for at least six months. The last thing they wrote, according to two-thirds of those surveyed, was a hastily scribbled note, a shopping list, or a reminder meant for their eyes only.[6] And in China many adults are forgetting how to draw basic Chinese characters because they type far more often than they write by hand. Many Chinese children are no longer even learning the characters. Calligraphy classes have been widely dropped in favor of science and math. Teachers themselves are less and less inclined to write, deferring instead to mouse-clicked lesson plans displayed on tablets or computers.[7]

And let's face it, who can honestly recall receiving anything *personal or handwritten* in the mail during the past several years other than a random birthday card or thank-you note? While many digital immigrants may find this disturbing, most digital natives are unlikely to bat an eye. The natives ask: Why would I want to write by hand, let alone

< 23 >

in cursive, when typing is so much faster and easier to read? But to an older person, for whom a handwritten thank-you note is the epitome of courtesy, it may well appear that basic handwritten notes are going into the same pile as 8-track tapes.

Gen Y versus the Board of Education

New York University professor and *Huffington Post* blogger Mary Quigley wrote in a July 2012 blog:

> In a journalism seminar last semester, a professor strolled around the class of 15 students as they discussed a reading. The prof noticed one student typing furiously on her laptop so she peered over her shoulder. "What are you doing?" the prof asked. "I am buying airline tickets," replied the student. "No you're not," said the prof as she shut the laptop, leaving the student aghast.[8]

As it turns out, this professor had previously won numerous awards for teaching excellence. Her classroom was *not* boring! Nonetheless, if one considers the neurobiological development of active young people today, whose brains experience constant rewards for multitasking, this teacher's understanding of her student's educational needs may soon be as obsolete as transistor radios! The simple fact is that digital natives are used to multitasking. They listen to a professor and take a note or two while simultaneously checking their email, updating their Facebook page, texting their friends, and, if the need arises, purchasing an airline ticket. Whether one's productivity is increased or diminished by doing several things at once has yet to be studied in those individuals who've grown up doing just that. Nevertheless, it is clear that multitasking has become the accepted norm for digital natives. One further conclusion that may be worth noting is this: the educational advantage offered in the past to those people who could sit and quietly focus on one teacher and one subject for several hours at a time may fast be disappearing. On the other hand, those individuals who can't focus (like those with attention deficit disorder) and need constant multiple sources of stim-

< 24 >

ulus to remain focused may now have an evolutionary advantage. For those who work, learn, and engage primarily in the digital universe, the ability to superficially focus on multiple things simultaneously, without any one taking precedence—what we now view as a classroom problem—may well be an asset in the very near future.

Of course, many digital immigrant (read: older) teachers are, for the most part, perfectly capable of texting, emailing, conducting online research, downloading music, socializing, and doing pretty much anything their students do online—be it with a laptop, a smartphone, or any other device. However, the concept of doing these things *while an authority figure is speaking* is completely foreign to them. They didn't grow up in the land of perpetual connectivity. As Quigley writes, "Gen Y views digital connectivity as a basic right…. Office, school, home and elsewhere, Gen Y goes online whenever and however they want."[9] Gen Y's predecessors don't get it. In fact, they often judge this behavior as disrespectful and rude.

Educator Mark Prensky hypothesizes that digital immigrant teachers may need to learn new ways to communicate fluently with digital natives in their own "language" to be more effective educators. Today, educators at virtually every level of learning have done so (or attempted such) by incorporating web lessons and other online activities into their teaching plans. In the fall of 2013, The Los Angeles Unified School District (the largest in the United States), rolled out a program that will ultimately provide an Apple iPad, preloaded with grade appropriate books and educational software to every student in that district (now over 620,000 students) and every educator (over 45,000). No more hardbound text books and written lesson plans? We're nearly there. Furthermore, many instructors have embraced online education themselves. On LinkedIn, a popular discussion forum for professionals of all ilks (including teachers), there are, at the time of this writing, approximately 30,000 education-related discussion groups. The Technology in Education group alone has nearly 27,000 members.

Furthermore, college courses taught entirely online have been available (on a small scale) for over a decade, while several universities now provide online graduate programs. And over the past few years,

< 25 >

we have begun to experience a global tsunami in online education—from grade school through graduate school. For example, a dozen major universities recently joined in a venture sponsored by Coursera—a company founded by two Stanford University computer science professors—to create one hundred massive open online courses (MOOCs). These offerings are expected to attract millions of students worldwide in a wide range of subjects, including poetry, history, and medicine. For one prototype course in artificial intelligence, (AI), offered by Stanford University in 2011, over 160,000 students from 190 countries signed up. Although only a small percentage of these online students actually completed the course, the overall level of interest is more than a little impressive. Writing about this educational experience, the *New York Times* gushed, "MOOCs are likely to be a game changer, opening higher education to hundreds of millions of people."[10] By November 2012, Coursera had expanded to include 33 university partners and had enrolled over 2 million students. Its most successful class, "How to Reason and Argue," attracted over 180,000 students. At about the same time, Harvard and MIT announced they would each put up $30 million to launch edX, a nonprofit venture offering courses from Ivy League universities. Yet another MOOC, Udacity, had 475,000 users by late 2012.[11]

Most professors likely find it mind-boggling and overwhelming, yet also perhaps extremely attractive, to be able to teach tens of thousands of students at the same time. And this could become a reality sooner rather than later, as some universities consider offering credit for Coursera courses. In the future, online classes may be combined with live lessons to provide traditional interaction between faculty and students in addition to online lectures. In many ways, the meaning of the phrase "going to college" is rapidly changing—especially for individuals who do not have the time or the financial resources to attend a traditional, brick-and-mortar university.

Even within traditional educational institutions teachers are today interacting with students (and parents) through digital media—emails, texts, classroom websites, and so on. College professors who used to find their offices crowded with students during their designated office hours now sit at their desks researching, writing, or planning future

< 26 >

lessons during this same time period. Many will digitally interact with their students in real time over computers, phones, notebooks, and laptops via Skype, FaceTime, instant messaging, and other Voice over Internet Protocol (VoIP) technologies. Teachers receive texts and emails from students at all hours of the day and night. And while technology has made professors more accessible than ever to their students, actual face-to-face interactions occur less frequently. How this change will affect relationships between professors and students and ultimately the learning process itself remains to be seen—especially over the long-term.

Educators differ in their approach to students using digital technology in the classroom. Mary Quigley, the *Huffington Post* blogger, comments:

> In my college classroom, I don't allow cell phones but do permit laptops on the assumption that students will use them to take notes and to pull up the assigned readings (the days of handouts are over). While some are writing down key points or referring to readings, a good number are also surfing the Internet (sometimes to share updates on the topic du jour), finishing an assignment for my class or another, checking email and logging on to Facebook. On my last day of class this spring, I asked my students about why they feel the need to be online constantly, even in class. One admitted that if the browser was open he felt compelled to surf; "I'm addicted," he said. While several students complained that it was distracting to sit next to other students who are on Facebook typing away, they didn't want to say anything. Another student tried to justify checking her email occasionally during class for "important" messages; of course when you're 19, an "important" message can be anything from Jessica Simpson giving birth, to a Supreme Court ruling, to an internship posting.[12]

While some experts believe it is possible to successfully digitally multitask in the classroom and elsewhere, others vehemently disagree. But the fact is to date there is simply not enough evidence-based re-

< 27 >

search, particularly studies about Gen Y and Gen Z, to know if digital natives who've grown up multitasking will develop the skills to be as productive or perhaps even more productive than previous generations. Whereas most baby boomers would likely argue that it is virtually impossible to carry on an in-person conversation while simultaneously typing on another topic, their *belief* that a person cannot divide his or her attention in that manner does not mean that people cannot *evolve* to do just that—where required. And it is equally likely that most Millennials would disagree with the boomers' point of view. So, are the brains of digital natives literally developing differently than the brains of older generations? This seems quite likely considering the early developmental stage at which children now begin using digital communication technology, but it is also too soon to know. What is certain is that sociologists, educators, communication experts, and brain researchers are keeping a close eye on this possibility. What we do know now is that classrooms—indeed, education as a whole—have been altered permanently by the digital revolution. Whether you feel that these changes are for the better or worse depends, to a large extent, on when you were born.

The Workplace Divide

Digital immigrants and digital natives increasingly face a generation gap in the workplace as well. In part, this stems from differing generational values related to concepts like "respect for authority," "respect for the workplace," what defines a "solid work ethic," and "communal productivity." Yet the bulk of this current workplace divide appears to stem from differing uses of and reliance upon new communications and documentation technologies.

Up until very recently, workplaces were usually populated by only two generations at a time. While these two generations may not have always liked or respected each other, they *knew* each other. There weren't a lot of surprises. When the younger generation "misbehaved," the older generation recognized what was going on and dealt with it effectively because, as parents, they had raised that younger generation. The older generation was usually able to *push the right buttons* to get the desired result from younger employees because they were the ones who installed

< 28 >

the buttons. And when the older generation got cranky, the younger generation understood. They'd seen the same occasional crankiness in their parents and teachers while they were growing up, so they knew what it was all about and, more important, what to do to smooth things over.

Today, however, as people are remaining in the workforce longer, three and sometimes even four generations are working together in a typical business. The age and experience gap between a semi retired Silent Generation senior manager and a Gen Y worker bee can be immense. These two sets of individuals have vastly different cultural references, are motivated by different things, use the tools of the workplace differently, and, most important, communicate differently—not only in terms of the language they use but also in the ways they use it. Members of widely spaced, multiple generations may struggle to recognize, let alone understand, the older or younger person's perspective because the generational unfamiliarity is simply too deep. Their generational norms are too far apart to fully understand each other or to communicate fluently with one another. For instance, to the Silent Generation the phrase "communication skills" by definition means the ability to speak eloquently and to write organized, grammatically correct formal documents. To the Gen Y worker that same phrase means fluency with email, texting, social media, smartphone apps, websites, and other recently developed communications technologies. Same phrase, vastly different interpretation—yet both will likely show up on a résumé.

Older and younger workers can often fail not only to recognize and acknowledge that a simple phrase might mean two completely different things, but also to accept the validity of the other generation's workplace values and ethics. For instance, most older workers were educated and trained in what could be considered hierarchical or "top-down" work environments. Here, the boss is to be unquestionably respected, while workers do what they're told without question. In such environments an older boss is much more likely to communicate by writing a formal memo than shouting across the room. Conversely, younger workers are more at home with a more collaborative model—with everyone contributing to the direction taken, giving, receiving, validating,

< 29 >

and questioning everyone's ideas and contributions. Furthermore, Gen Y workers tend to communicate in whatever way seems fastest—text messaging, emailing, or walking into a private office unannounced. This is an approach that people from older generations sometimes find offensive or disrespectful. These misunderstandings—and *misunderstandings* are exactly what they are—can cause a great deal of unintended and unnecessary intergenerational workplace tension. Furthermore, people from different generations are often motivated by different rewards in the workplace. Whereas older workers often look for praise, raises, and promotions, younger workers are typically more interested in extra time off and other "quality of life" perks. Neither generation's attitude appears to be any better or worse than the other's; they're just different. Yet that difference creates conflict.

A major chasm appears to be forming in the workplace between digital natives and digital immigrants regarding all things technological. Some experts contend that baby boomers and Gen Ys, in particular, have increasingly clashing values and misaligned worldviews, and a 2011 poll by the Society for Human Resource Management found 47 percent of Gen Y workers felt older managers (boomers) were resistant to change, whereas 33 percent of boomers decried Gen Y's informality, need for structure, and lack of respect for authority.[13] Furthermore, the study found that 38 percent of older workers had concerns about younger employees' "inappropriate use or excessive reliance on technology." Conversely, 31 percent of younger workers thought their older managers had an "aversion to technology."[14] A study canvassing 3,800 Gen Y workers in fifteen countries further supported this conflict, finding Gen Y employees "have an expectation—not a hope—that they will be able to use their own mobile smartphones and tablets for work-related activities. In fact, that expectation [is] the driving force for a critical mass of users who maintain they would go or have gone against company policy in order to use their own mobile device for work. And, like it or not, *organizations* [emphasis added] will have to adapt." This insistence by Gen Y on using their own technology can negatively impact both workplace environments and company security, but it is not likely to change. Gen Y is here to stay, and so is the technology that Gen Y loves.

< 30 >

As the study concluded, "It is businesses rather than workers who must adapt."[15] In many ways, the BYOD (bring your own device) movement is similar to the early days of workplace computers, when employees suddenly wanted to toss aside paper in lieu of Lotus spreadsheets and Macs for desktop publishing. So IT departments adapted, and business moved forward, becoming more efficient in almost every way.

But how are digital immigrants to survive and successfully negotiate a workplace that doesn't uniformly respect or appreciate their values? Read below for some clues.

Workplace Management For Digital Immigrants

- Take the time to learn about new technology, accepting that in many ways it offers potential improvement and in all ways it's here to stay (until replaced by something even newer). Those who struggle with new technology are well served by pairing them with a "reverse mentor"—that is, a digital native to act as guide and interpreter.
- Allow, even encourage the coexistence of differing work ethics, recognizing that people from younger generations may be more interested than their older counterparts in achieving a healthy work-life balance—which often includes telecommuting and flexible hours. Consider the possibility that this doesn't mean young people are lazy or unmotivated; it just means they approach work differently.
- Learn and accept the new forms of business communication, understanding that face-to-face communication (scheduled meetings) may not be in line with the much more immediate ways in which younger generations communicate—using IMs, texts, and Skype.

Unfortunately, today many older workers are not coping well with new and evolving technologies. In a recent *Huffington Post* article, human resources management consultant Dr. Linda Gravett states, "I've had so many Boomers say to me, I'm not going to learn how to text, I want to talk to someone face-to-face doggone it and I'm going to track them down till I find them. I say … if you want to communicate with people across all age groups then learn how to text, learn how to instant

< 31 >

message, get out of your comfort zone and your rigidity that every kind of communication must be either by letter or email or even face-to-face because that isn't necessarily practical."[16]

Technology and Politics

Do digital natives and digital immigrants differ politically? One school of thought says digital natives are (or will become) more responsible citizens than their predecessors by using their technological expertise to exert social change. With their technological know-how, the theory goes, younger people can communicate more quickly and more expertly than their predecessors. And there are certainly examples that support this, such as the 2008 U.S. presidential election in which digital natives voted for Barack Obama (who campaigned heavily online via Facebook and Twitter) by a two-to-one margin, while digital immigrants were essentially evenly split between Obama and John McCain. Whether Gen Ys voted for Obama because he did a better job of communicating with them or because he better represented their political ideals remains open for debate. More than likely the result was a combination of both factors.

As the *Economist* stated in 2010:

> There is a feeling of superficiality about much online youth activism. Any teenager can choose to join a Facebook group supporting the opposition in Iran or the liberation of Tibet, but such engagement is likely to be shallow. A recent study by the Pew Research Center, an American think-tank, found that Internet users aged 18-24 were the least likely of all age groups to e-mail a public official or make an online political donation. But when it came to using the web to share political news or join political causes on social networks, they were far ahead of everyone else. Rather than genuinely being more politically engaged, they may simply wish to broadcast their activism to their peers. [There] may be less going on here than meets the eye.[17]

Of course, the same thing could be said about baby boomer activists in the 1960s. Were most boomers attending rallies and sit-ins because

< 32 >

they fully understood the causes, or because it seemed like the groovy thing to do? Once again, the answer is likely some combination of the two.

So far, the political split between Gen Y and older generations has not played out with the same visible acrimony as the gap between the boomer generation of the 1960s and 1970s and its predecessors. This, however, may change. After all, many current public policies work to the benefit of older generations at the expense of younger people. In Great Britain, young people have responded to this disparity by forming the Intergenerational Foundation, (www.if.org.uk), an organization created to publicize and redress their many grievances. Their slogan? "Fairness for Future Generations." These young activists are lobbying online rather than taking to the streets as boomers once did, but they're nonetheless getting the message out.

In the United States, Generations Y and Z will soon rule the political roost. As Morley Winograd and Michael D. Hais wrote in a 2012 *National Journal* article, "At 95 million, Millennials [Gen Y] are the largest American generation ever. By 2020 they will comprise more than one in three eligible voters. Sooner or later, those numbers, and the unity of belief that the millennial generation has so far brought to politics, will allow that generation to reshape the United States, first as voters and then as the nation's leaders. The way in which boomers and seniors react to the growing presence of Millennials, and the younger generation's distinctive beliefs and experiences, will determine the difficulty of the transition from the old America to the new."[18]

The "Friends and Family" Plan

Virtually everything discussed in this chapter in terms of the "generation gap" between digital natives and digital immigrants centers around the technology used for communicating and "staying connected." And though under acknowledged by the generations that have come before, *no group in history* has been more interconnected than Generations Y and Z! In 2009, more than half of American teens logged on to a social media website more than once per day, with nearly a quarter of teens logging on to their favorite social media site ten or more times per day.[19] That

< 33 >

same year, a study by the Pew Internet and American Life Project found that three quarters of U.S. teens owned a cell phone, with 88 percent of them texting regularly. Boys typically sent and received thirty texts per day; girls sent and received eighty per day. Girls age fourteen to seventeen typically sent at least one hundred texts per day. A more recent Pew study shows the median number of daily texts among teens age twelve to seventeen has risen from fifty texts per day in 2009 to sixty texts per day in 2012, with older teens, boys, and African Americans leading the increase, though girls ages fourteen to seventeen remain the most avid texters, still averaging well over one hundred per day.[20] The survey also revealed that texting is now the primary mode of daily communication between teens and their friends and family, far surpassing phone calls, face-to-face interactions, and email.[21]

Consider the opening sentences of Associated Press writer Martha Irvine's June 2012 article "Is Texting Ruining the Art of Conversation?"

> Anna Schiferl hadn't even rolled out of bed when she reached for her cellphone and typed a text to her mom one recent Saturday. Mom was right downstairs in the kitchen. The text? Anna wanted cinnamon rolls for breakfast. Soon after, the 13-year-old could hear Mom's voice echoing through the house. "Anna," Joanna Schiferl called, "if you want to talk to me, you come downstairs and see me!" Anna laughs about it now. "I was kind of being lazy," the teen from suburban Chicago concedes. "I know that sounds horrible." Well, maybe not horrible, but certainly increasingly typical.[22]

The fact is digital natives are often more comfortable texting than talking—live or on the phone. And this may not be such a bad thing.

Brad, a tech-savvy member of Gen X, recently flew from his West Coast home to visit family in the Midwest, including his parents, sister, and her three teenage children. He'd not seen the kids in more than a year. Brad writes:

> We had three generations at dinner one night. My parents, my sister and me, and my sister's three kids—ages 17, 14, and 11.

< 34 >

I keep up with my sister's frequent Facebook posts, so I know what my two nieces and my nephew are up to, and sometimes I'll send one of them a congratulatory text for making the honor roll or doing well in baseball or a dance competition. But I don't post much on Facebook, so they don't know a whole lot about me—only what my sister tells them, and she's pretty busy so that's probably only the basics. While I was catching up with the adults at the table during dinner I felt my phone buzz, informing me I'd just gotten a text. I checked and saw it was from Kris, the 17-year-old. "What is it that you do?" she texted. I turned to her and said, "For a living, you mean?" She nodded. So I briefly explained to her and the rest of the family my career as a writer. They asked a few questions, which I answered as best I could, and then we moved on to greener pastures. Later in the meal my phone buzzed again—another text from Kris.

Kris: "Are you gay?"
Brad: "Yes. Is that OK?"
Kris: "Yeah, we're all cool with it, but your mom and dad don't like to talk about it."
Brad: "They're from a different generation."
Kris: "Tell me about it. I just wanted you to know that David, Ashley, and I know, and we love you."
Brad: "Thanks. I love you too."

The most meaningful exchange of my entire five-day visit occurred during a family dinner—in private, via text.

Would Uncle Brad and Kris's exchange have ever happened before texting existed? "Probably not," says Brad. Even if Kris had been able to find a moment alone with him, it's likely she would have struggled to approach her uncle so directly. For Kris, the "digital buffer" of texting made this very intimate exchange much easier, and yet for Brad the conversation was no less meaningful because it was texted.

In summary, we offer the following overriding concept: human interaction and communication may be no less meaningful or productive

< 35 >

simply because it is in digital form. And further, it is this concept that separates most digital immigrants from most digital natives. Older people, based both on a lifetime of experience as well as their earliest developmental experiences of social interaction, more often want and need face-to-face interpersonal interactions, or at least a telephone exchange, where they can listen to another person's voice. Younger people, on the other hand, seem to feel that communication is communication, no matter the format, and why wait to see (or talk to) someone when you can text them right now and get an instant response? They ask, "Why would you be *disconnected* when you can post on Facebook, text, and tweet to let your friends and family know what you're up to, and they can do the same to keep in touch with you? Why not stay connected?"

Consider another example in Irvine's article, this one about how Lisa Auster-Gussman, a senior at the University of Richmond in Virginia, uses technology to stay in touch with people in her life:

> For her, there are simply particular tools she uses to communicate, depending on the recipient. Email is for professors, yes. Phone calls and maybe the occasional texts are for parents, if the parents know how to do the latter. "But I don't communicate much with older people. So much of my life is set up over text." ... Meanwhile, last summer, when she was away from her boyfriend, she went days without talking to him on the phone but texted him several times a day. "But I felt like I was talking to him all day, every day," she said.[23]

Lisa's experience is relatively common among digital natives. However, it's difficult to fathom many sixty-year-old boomers, for example, thinking that "texting and checking in via Twitter" feels the same as talking face-to-face. And that is the crux of the interpersonal communications generation gap—*live versus electronic communication, analog versus digital*. Is the split a big deal? Does it make a difference *how* we communicate? The answers to these questions are, not surprisingly, both yes and no. Had Uncle Brad been unwilling or unable to communicate via text he would have missed out on an incredibly powerful conversation

< 36 >

with his niece. On the other hand, if he hadn't been willing to show up in person, he would have missed out on some wonderful moments with his parents. For him, the method of communication doesn't matter much. "I prefer face-to-face," he says, "but there are definitely times when texting is faster and easier." For his parents, though, and also for his niece Kris, talking versus texting *does* matter.

Ultimately, the most successful communicators among us are able and willing to engage others utilizing whatever media is most useful at the time, while recognizing the most appropriate circumstance for each method. They neither avoid nor insist on a particular mode of interaction. Instead, they work hard to make sure their message is heard by whomever they're trying to reach. They assimilate. According to educator Timothy VanSlyke, "cultural assimilation rarely entails a wholesale abandonment of previous customs or practices; rather, it typically involves a flexible process of negotiation and adaptation, wherein certain elements of both cultures are retained in a new combination with one another."[24] In other words, the most successful communicators today accept and even embrace the idea that they need to live in and communicate fluently in both the digital native and digital immigrant worlds. They evolve *with* technology.

Unfortunately, for those entrenched in the idea that "the way it has always been is *the best way*," this kind of cultural assimilation is not an easy task, and therefore it feels easier to judge and avoid than embrace. This may be why the current digital native–immigrant generation gap is not as volatile as previous generation gaps, such as the openly acrimonious split between the baby boomers and their parents in the 1960s and 1970s. And it may well be that the roots of what currently appears to be a relatively serene generational divide lies in the fact that older and younger generations don't even know what their differences are since they're rarely sharing ideas in the same space! Perhaps we lack proper discourse because digital natives and digital immigrants aren't "in the same room," thereby avoiding vociferous disagreement yet sacrificing mutual understanding.

< 37 >

CHAPTER TWO

The Internet: Where Everyone Can Be Heard

The Internet is becoming the town square for the global village of tomorrow.
—Bill Gates

Digital technology has created positive revolutionary change. In less than half a decade, innovations like Facebook, with over 1 billion members, and Twitter, with over 300 million subscribers, have made possible *real-time interactions* with an increasingly wider and more diverse group of people than any one person could have ever previously connected with. In the past, even if someone's appearance in a movie or on television reached many people, those were at best static, one-sided communication venues. Social media today not only allows a person to reach millions of people simultaneously, they allow us to *mutually share* uncensored ideas and information—communication now occurs as quickly and efficiently with those across the globe as with friends just around the corner.

Support groups and educational forums also now come together online IRT (in real time), without anyone having to ride the subway, drive, hop on a plane, or even suffer through a conference call. Short-term and ongoing peer support for common concerns related to every imaginable kind of financial, social, work, or personal problem can easily be located online in the form of educational forums, parenting support groups, and Twelve Step recovery meetings. Today, we have less of a need to travel anywhere beyond our own living rooms to obtain helpful counsel, support, and direction. As a result, there should be more time available for personal development, creativity, and quality

< 39 >

moments with loved ones. The reality, of course, is that the extra time is often used for work.

For many people, adolescents in particular, consistent online contact with peers can increase self-esteem via the continuously communicated approval and acceptance of others.[1] For some individuals, particularly those who are by nature less social, the Internet can be a BFF (best friend forever), allowing them to build connections and relationships without experiencing the discomfort of in-person interaction. When online, those with social inhibitions can connect with other people while remaining in their comfort zone. They are physically alone yet communicating with others with added time for thoughtful self-expression and less anxiety about being put on the spot. Oftentimes, shy people can project online an outgoing personality very different from who they are in the real world; this phenomenon is so common that it has earned its own name: electronic extroversion.[2] For such people, life online offers freedom from an activity they may have previously experienced as a painful burden (in-person social interaction), as it helps them gain control over the speed and access of their human connections. This evolving way to connect presents a significant advantage for passive and shy people, and even those with an irrational fear of open or public places (agoraphobia), as a means of growing more connections and feeling "part of" the community.

These are just a few ways in which digital technology continues to advance our world. We see daily the positive effects related to information gathering and processing, political and social activism, diagnosing and managing illness, communicating with friends and family, and developing new relationships—including intimate partnerships.

Global Information Gathering: Reformatted

Consider the following story: In 1989, Jessica, then a bright and inquisitive college student, landed the summer job of her dreams as a research assistant to a journalist who was then writing a book about Latin America. Every morning Jessica left her house, drove to work, and reported to her boss, who would give her a list of research questions to explore. She would then drive to the local university library, where she spent the

< 40 >

bulk of her day literally foraging through the library's stacks, card files, encyclopedias, microfiche, and other materials in order to gather the requested information. Until very recently, research work was considered long, lonely, and tedious. And depending on the information needed and the skill of the person gathering it, the process had the potential to produce inaccurate, misleading, and/or incomplete sets of data.

Contrast Jessica's experience with a similar assignment given to another student, Katy, just last year to find information about the 1989 *Exxon Valdez* oil spill. In less than thirty minutes online, Katy found out exactly how many miles of beach were polluted, how many fish and birds were killed, and every other major detail of that sad ecological event. Her brief search even produced recently declassified U.S. government documents and internal Exxon corporation communications—material that in the past would likely have required a trip to Washington and/or Texas to acquire. In 1989, for Jessica this work would have taken weeks, perhaps even months of phone calls, letters, and travel, but today Katy needed only half an hour!

Digital access to information has made Jessica's old job a relic of a bygone era (in a mere twenty-five years), bringing about a sea change in our ability to quickly gather and process information from multiple sources. This newfound efficiency leaves us with extra time for broader and more in-depth research—research that can be readily verified using any number of reputable online sources. This improvement is in part courtesy of incredibly effective Internet search engines (such as Google, Yahoo, and Bing) that can immediately locate and bring forth a wealth of resources.

Wikipedia

Gathering and maintaining information has become an increasingly collaborative venture among government, business, and the private sector, undertaken because it brings with it clear advantages to all concerned.

Without doubt, the most useful and successful online collaborative information-gathering venture to date is Wikipedia—a free international online encyclopedia that is probably the single most commonly used general reference site in the world. Wikipedia is, essentially, a fluid com-

< 41 >

pilation of articles written and edited by a worldwide conglomeration of volunteers. According to Wikipedia, the site has approximately 100,000 regular contributors, 22 million articles, and, as of February 2013, editions in 285 languages.[3] It is the largest encyclopedia ever created and it evolved from idea to fruition in less than five years.

Founded in 2001 by Jimmy Wales and Larry Sanger, Wikipedia was initially an offshoot of a planned online encyclopedia to be authored by multiple experts—in other words, a traditional encyclopedia made available on the Internet. For the offshoot, Wales and Sanger sought to obtain additional information on multiple subjects by creating an open-source or "wiki" website. The word *wiki* itself refers to a website that allows anyone to add, delete, or revise content.

As authorship of its articles is not limited to recognized experts and because anyone can edit an article, Wikipedia has been criticized for occasional inaccuracies, misrepresentations, and possible biases. Students and other researchers are told not to rely on Wikipedia. However, a non-scientific report published in the journal *Nature* comparing science articles in Wikipedia and the traditional *Encyclopedia Britannica* found that the two publications had a strikingly similar level of accuracy.[4] Of course, on Wikipedia there is always the risk of someone deliberately inserting false information into an article, but Wikipedia reports that the median time to correct inaccuracies is a mere three to five minutes. What helps maintain accuracy is that all contributions are expected to be supported by published and verifiable sources. Notably, the average contributor to Wikipedia today is in his or her mid-twenties—one among many examples of young people both creating and using new technologies and media.

Crowdsourcing, Crowd-Purchasing, and Crowdfunding ... Oh My!

Wikipedia is a superb example of the phenomenon recently termed *crowdsourcing*—using the collaborative resources of many people to accomplish a task or solve a problem.[5] The term evolved from the word *outsourcing*, but in contrast to traditional forms of outsourcing (where a specific group of people outside the United States, such as customer service representatives, are hired to perform a specific task (at a lower

< 42 >

wage), crowdsourcing distributes a large task via open call to anyone (usually without pay).

This type of collaborative methodology actually has a well-documented, pre-high-tech history dating back to the late nineteenth century. At that time, Dr. James Murray, a professor in Oxford, England, conceived and launched a collaborative project aimed at creating a major new dictionary of the English language. Over many years, unpaid strangers perused books on behalf of Murray's project, each volunteer indexing a word or words, suggesting definitions, and providing quotations demonstrating various uses. Thousands of people mailed in hundreds of thousands of documents to Murray. The ultimate result was the huge *Oxford English Dictionary*, published in stages beginning in 1884 and still in use today.[6]

Of course, crowdsourcing as a strategy can now be implemented much more rapidly and efficiently than in the past, while also drawing on a much larger pool of participants. It can be and has been used in the form of competitions (some offering prizes) to find solutions to mathematical, technical, architectural, and other problems. A great site for this is FoldIt (http://fold.it), where users play carefully designed puzzle games, the results of which are utilized by the scientists who set up the games to better understand concepts like protein structure and organ design. As it turns out, humans are much better at pattern recognition and puzzle solving than computer programs, and the combined efforts of players recently helped solve an HIV/AIDS-related problem that had confused researchers for more than a decade![7] Then there are noncompetitive websites, such as Ask.com that request site visitors provide answers to questions on topics posed by other site visitors; the reward is often pride and enjoyment in knowing that your answer may help others, along with fulfillment of the very human desire to be acknowledged for one's skills and knowledge. On some sites, people earn "points" for answering questions and those points give them special privileges.

One of the more interesting recent examples of crowdsourcing is a 2009 British Parliament expenses scandal. Essentially, certain members of British Parliament (MPs) had been filing, for years, bogus expense claims for everything from personal gardening fees to, in one case, a

< 43 >

"floating duck island." When rumors of the abuse broke, the government responded by releasing more than a million unsorted MP expense reports as electronic documents, likely thinking that no one would have the desire or wherewithal to sift through the mess and, therefore, the potential scandal would eventually blow over. The *Guardian*, which had been covering the story, knew it didn't have enough manpower to sort the morass of documents itself, so it hired a software developer to create a website, Investigate Your MP's Expenses, on which anyone could examine the documents. Much to the dismay of those cheating on their business expenses, in just three days 20,000 people had examined 170,000 of the documents! By the time the smoke cleared, dozens of MPs were forced to resign, some of them facing legal consequences for their actions.[8]

Relying on similar group-think, and economies-of-scale models, retail businesses now routinely use websites such as Groupon.com to offer discounts on meals, vacations, car washes, and other services, provided a minimum number of people sign up to purchase that item or service. This is called *crowd-purchasing*. Another variant is *crowdfunding*, in which a nonprofit or similar project can be funded by requesting small donations from a large number of people who may be interested in seeing that particular project completed.

The Doctor Is In 24/7 ... (Online)

In 1985, when medical doctors wanted to know more about an unusual medical condition encountered in their practice they had to go to great lengths to obtain that information—doing an extensive library search, calling or writing (by "snail mail") medical colleagues and organizations specializing in related disorders, and perhaps asking a medical journal to post an announcement about the condition. All this took a lot of effort and time, often months or even longer. Today, in contrast, physicians can post a one-sentence query online and acquire information from all over the world in a few days or even a few hours.

And it's not just doctors seeking answers. Medical patients and their loved ones can find needed information through online postings. For instance, on June 29, 2012, Simon Turkajli created a Facebook page

< 44 >

describing his wife's unusual and, to that point, undiagnosed condition. Within a week, he was receiving over 1,000 opinions a day from around the world. As a result, doctors evaluated his wife for a potentially rare tumor.[9] Instantaneous access to millions of people and to almost unlimited data has resulted in unprecedented, ever-evolving options for medical diagnosis, treatment, and research, especially in the case of bizarre or unusual conditions.

Just a few years ago, Jennifer, a medical doctor, sustained a low-impact fracture of the femur (thighbone), the strongest bone in the body, while simply shifting weight from one leg to another on a crowded subway train. Over time, Jennifer came to believe the cause of this uncommon injury to be long-term use of Fosamax®, a drug that is frequently used to strengthen bones in both women and men with some bone loss. Jennifer then subsequently wrote and published a case report about her experience.[10]

Since that time, she has continually received emails from others with similar fractures. Eventually she created a database and LISTSERV to provide email support and information to those seeking help. Thanks to the Internet, she was able to collect detailed data from eighty-one patients who had suffered similar injuries after long-term Fosamax® use—enough to draw useful conclusions about the length of use of the medication, symptoms before the fracture, complications, and long-term outcome.

At the time of this writing, over 160 women and men who have been similarly affected by Fosamax® have reached out to her for help and information. And she has twice been asked to testify about her experience and findings at the Food and Drug Administration (FDA) in Washington, DC. Without the easy, worldwide access the Internet provides, she would never have been able to form her "femur fracture" support group, nor would she have been able to conduct this study, which is today effecting positive change in the medical community.

< 45 >

> **AUTHORS' NOTE—MEDICAL INFORMATION ONLINE**
>
> Please note that the authors are not advocating that anyone attempt to obtain a conclusive medical diagnosis or treatment plan via Internet searches. Even on the best medical and psychiatric websites, online information can be conflicting, inaccurate, and misleading—especially for those desperate to reduce their symptoms or find a cure. It's dangerous and incorrect to believe that if it's written online, it must be true. Instead, consider the Internet a resource to be used toward finding a knowledgeable clinician in your area, a support group, an overview of the potential diagnoses of the problem, clues for further research, and, most importantly, to become better prepared with useful questions to ask your doctor.

Who Needs Rats When You've Got People?

Science in general, not just the medical community, is benefiting from the crowdsourcing concept. For instance, one of the most popular sites for scientific research, Amazon's Mechanical Turk (www.mturk.com), has a paid worldwide workforce of over 500,000 people, of whom 40 percent are from the United States. For a pittance (about $1.40 per hour), these individuals can participate in online research projects, including psychological research and other experiments that interest them.[11] In the past, the most accessible experimental subjects were college students taking a course on the topic being studied. Now, large-scale studies involving a much wider array of test subjects can be done more easily and less expensively than in the past. This research method is rapidly expanding. Already, according to Google Scholar, there are over 3,000 published research papers that have relied on crowdsourcing to collect data.

Political and Social Change Begins Online

Take a moment to imagine the time and energy it took (pre-Internet) for a political, social, or other activist group to reach out to large numbers of fellow citizens. They had to call or write contacts in multiple locations, put ads in newspapers wherever possible, gather a team of people to create and post flyers, or buy billboards. Often, they worked for years before their issue generated enough interest for them to be freely invited into the mass media (newspapers, radio, and television). Today,

< 46 >

in contrast, that same individual can quickly reach millions of people worldwide with a few tweets or sentences on Facebook, by posting an online petition, by uploading photos and an interview on YouTube, or by blogging. Now anyone with Internet access can affordably and effectively reach millions of people in very little time. Thanks to the Internet, the power of the individual to quickly reach out, influence others, and effect change has increased exponentially.

One example of this phenomenon is change.org, which distributes petitions for any nonprofit, crisis-related, or legal cause, often rapidly collecting many thousands of signatures (and sometimes donations), thereby encouraging social change. Founded in 2007, change.org has a membership of ten million people, two million of whom live outside the United States. So far, the site has launched 93,000 petitions and claims success in over 1,000 cases.[12] In late 2011, for instance, Bank of America announced a new monthly five-dollar debit card fee in response to new consumer credit banking laws. Within a few days, a change.org member posted an online petition against this fee. Within a month, over 300,000 people had signed, eventually resulting in Bank of America rescinding the proposed charge.

The "Arab Spring" and Beyond

Internet-propelled change is worldwide. In January 2011, the first of a series of political revolutions in the Middle East and North Africa began in Tunisia, thanks to the widespread presence and use of social media, in particular Facebook and Twitter. About 850,000 active Facebook users in Tunisia (about 35 percent of the Tunisian population) were able to communicate with each other, even though traditional channels of communication such as radio and television had been cut off by the government.

After only a few months, following twenty-three years of tyrannical rule, Tunisian president Zine Ben Ali stepped down in response to pressure from protesters, most of them young people. Those who participated in an online survey within days of the revolution wrote comments such as:

< 47 >

- Tunisian media said nothing. [It] was people who spent hours in front of their screens sharing videos on Facebook which made them achieve the revolution.
- Facebook played the most important role in uncovering the truth hidden by national media sources in Tunisia.
- Facebook allowed the most rapid transmission of information and helped Tunisian users find that they shared the same views.[13]

Similar and still-evolving revolutions in places like Egypt and Syria have also been unquestionably sparked and maintained via social media. Today, some governments (such as North Korea, Cuba, and China) work very hard to maintain tight control of their national Internets, thus blocking the unlimited dissemination of information that can lead to rapid political change. However, they are unlikely to succeed for long.

In essence, the influence of government censorship is lessening daily. The Internet enables the rapid dissemination of a single photograph or video, such as the suicide of a desperate young man in Tunisia—the spark that ignited the Arab Spring—to millions of people *from a single smartphone*. As a result, it is no longer as easy as it was in the past to quash cultural events before they become widely known.

Women's Rights in Pakistan

The story of Malala Yousufzai, a young Pakistani girl, provides another example of the power of social media. In 2009, at the age of eleven, Malala began speaking out against Taliban rule and in favor of women's rights, particularly the right to receive an education. And she spoke out in much the same way any American girl would state her opinion—online. Malala started by writing a blog, using a pseudonym, for the BBC detailing her life under Taliban rule, including the fact that the Taliban had, at times, banned girls from attending school. The following summer the *New York Times* produced a documentary about her life, her anonymity was broken, and she rose in prominence. In one CNN interview, she stated: "I have the right of education. I have the right to play. I have the right to sing. I have the right to talk. I have the right to go to

< 48 >

market. I have the right to speak up!"[14] In October 2012, Malala was shot in the head and neck while returning from school—an attempted assassination by the Taliban. Amazingly, Malala survived and continued her crusade. She has since received Pakistan's first National Youth Peace Prize, been nominated for the International Children's Peace Prize, and become the youngest ever nominee for the Nobel Peace Prize.

Rural Protest in China Launches Massive Outcry

As amazing as it may seem, political and social change can occur even in the few countries whose governments still strongly attempt censorship and Internet control. For instance, in China in 2011, as authorities in a remote town prepared to destroy the home of a young woman who had refused to sell her house to facilitate major new construction, an online photo of the woman and her house spread throughout the country. It generated such a massive protest that authorities were forced to adjust their building plans so the house could be spared. And this is not an isolated incident. In August 2012, in the city of Qidong, an hour north of Shanghai, thousands of people assembled to protest the construction of an industrial waste pipeline. According to CNN reporter Fareed Zakaria:

> Despite the presence of scores of policemen, the protesters went wild. Hundreds entered and took over an entire government building. Many windows were smashed. At least two police officers were beaten up. … I would have expected Beijing to retaliate with great force. Instead, they caved in. The waste disposal project was abandoned, and the state-run *People's Daily* applauded the decision, saying, "A responsive government should create an inclusive environment for public opinion."[15]

The very same thing occurred a few weeks earlier in Shifang, a Chinese city 2,000 miles to the west. In fact, residents of Qidong said they were inspired by the success in Shifang. The protesters in both cities mobilized on Weibo (China's version of Twitter), which has 300 million users.[16] As Zakaria concluded, "Despite Beijing's best efforts at censor-

< 49 >

ship, the Internet has empowered and connected communist China's people in a way that could not have been envisioned a few years ago…. The Internet won't make China free, but technology does help the cause of individual liberty."[17]

In 1946, Great Britian Prime Minister Winston Churchill spoke of an Iron Curtain, an imaginary symbol of the isolation and separation from the West experienced by the people of Soviet controlled Eastern Europe. Could an "Iron Curtain" even exist in today's digital world? Not likely, at least in the long term. Communication leading to major political shifts now stems in great part from the existence of the Internet. Thus, our relationship with digital communications technology is sowing the seeds of a truly global community. Today we are able to gather and disseminate information in real time with minimal interference. We can share goals, plans, and information among ourselves and whomever else we wish. We are able to collaborate with people all over the world to politically problem solve, influence governments, and even topple corrupt and/or abusive regimes.

Defusing Racial and Religious Prejudice

The Internet has also fostered increased insight into, as well as respect and tolerance of, differences between people, thereby diminishing cultural class and racial prejudice. In this vein, a Jewish colleague recently stated over lunch, "In 1978, when I left Boston to attend college in South Carolina, one of my classmates, who came from the Deep South, told me that she had never met a Jew before. She said then, at nineteen years old, that until meeting me she believed what her family and church had taught her as a child, that all Jews had horns hidden under their hair and this was the reason that Jewish men wear yarmulkes on their heads." Although this admission may seem startling or even silly to us today, this girl from the Deep South had no prior reason to doubt this misinformation. For someone who had never before spent time with anyone who wasn't Christian, this was an easy prejudice to maintain.

Thirty-five years later, such a conclusion would seem unlikely, as digital natives (and immigrants) are routinely exposed, via digital technology, to all sorts of information. Engaging with real people in real

< 50 >

time—a process that fosters both empathy and understanding has always been the most effective way to defuse prejudicial and uninformed beliefs. As such, the many connections and relationships now formed through social media and online educational sites are helping to both foster tolerance and promote cultural understanding.

Defusing Sexual Prejudice

No ethnic, racial, or other subgroup has benefited more from Internet sociopolitical change than the lesbian, gay, bisexual, and transgender (LGBT) community. Keep in mind that as late as the 1970s the American Psychiatric Association's (APA) *Diagnostic and Statistical Manual of Mental Health Disorders* defined homosexuality as a mental illness requiring long-term, psychiatric treatment. In other words, homosexuality was viewed as a profound *mental illness* by no less an authority than the APA! Homosexual "conduct" was also illegal—an arrestable offense in most parts of the United States and in many other countries. The APA changed its stance in 1973, reclassifying same-sex sexual and romantic attractions as normal and positive variations in the spectrum of human sexuality. Other major mental health organizations followed suit.

Sadly, even though the APA and most other mental health organizations came to recognize LGBT behavior as normal prior to the dawn of the Internet, much of Western society did not. Consequently, gays and lesbians were still largely marginalized and treated as "less than" and defective. Many suffered from depression and severe anxiety brought about by familial and societal rejection/condemnation/ignorance of their sexual orientation.

Sherry, a lesbian now in her mid-fifties, describes her experience:

I grew up in an upper-middle-class home with loving parents and three brothers who treated me like a princess. What more could a girl ask for? Frankly, I was spoiled. So why was I so miserable? Why did I try to kill myself once when I was in high school, again while I was in college, and once more after I got married? It was because I was living a lie, and I thought I was the only one. I had never been attracted to the boys I dated, and

< 51 >

I wasn't attracted to the man I married. I was attracted to women, and no one talked about things like that back then. Once in a while someone might make a joke about an effeminate man, but the concept of a woman who liked other women just didn't seem possible. I went to therapy for years after the suicide attempts, and I never even mentioned it. None of my therapists ever asked, either! And then we got the Internet. One day, when no one else was home, I went online and found a bulletin board for women seeking women. I was shocked, and also delighted. I answered an ad, and a few days later I had my first sexual experience with another woman. For the first time in my life, I didn't feel alone and ashamed.

These days, thanks to the Internet, LGBT young people no longer need to grow up feeling like "they're the only one." They can go online and get all sorts of helpful and supportive information. Even heterosexual kids check these sites out, learning more about their LGBT friends and family members. They access information about other formerly "taboo" social topics as well, such as birth control and what constitutes "normal" teen behavior. In some respects, the Internet has taken over the parental "birds and bees" obligation. Of course, the Internet is not always accurate, especially when depicting porn as typical human behavior, but more on that later.

It's Ten O'Clock—Do You Know Where Your Children Are?

In the early 1970s there was a long-running American television campaign reminding parents to constantly be aware of where their children were. Were they with friends? Out playing? Possibly getting into trouble? The public service announcement ran during the late evening news, raising awareness with the catchphrase, "It's ten o'clock. Do you know where your children are?" Today, any parent whose child has a smartphone with a tracking app can geolocate that child simply by saying to their own app-enabled smartphone, "Find Mike." The phone then brings up a map with a blinking icon showing where the child's phone is in real time. While these apps can't yet determine if the child actually

< 52 >

has the phone with him or her or has left it somewhere, today most parents feel safer knowing they can "find" their children whenever needed.

In fact, there are now endless ways for parents and guardians to keep track of their charges. A grandmother who picks up her ten- and twelve-year-old granddaughters after school and spends the rest of the afternoon with them recently learned that her daughter routinely texts the girls within a few minutes after they are scheduled to meet in order to make sure they are indeed now with Grandma. And when children go away to summer camp or college, parents can provide support and emotional connection via email, texts, photos, IMs, and webcams. Furthermore, parents can learn a lot of things about their children thanks to the tendency of young people to overshare on social media sites. Parents of otherwise secretive teenagers find this especially useful.

We Need to Talk ...

One of the drawbacks of emailing and texting is that these forms of communication often do not convey the various subtle cues that help us determine a person's true meaning and intent (such as tone of voice or facial expression). This is why emoticons are so popular as they can be used to clarify the sender's emotional state. On the other hand, not having those cues may actually facilitate some communication, especially between people who tend to react negatively when face-to-face. Some readers may recall the 1979 film, *Kramer vs. Kramer,* about a recently divorced couple who, despite their mutual acrimony, must maintain regular contact because they have a young son. A recent story in the *New York Times,* "Kramer.com vs. Kramer.com," described how technology is providing divorced parents with useful and less confrontational ways to communicate.

> People don't want to talk to their exes because just the sound of their voice is irritating ... but [now] they can email. They can share an online calendar. Email and texting alone have practically revolutionized post-divorce family relationships. Email absolutely takes away the in-your-face aggravation and emotional side of joint custody.... You just write, "I want to pick up

< 53 >

Kimmy at 5, but I'm running late and will be there at 6." It's the best thing ever…. When relationships deteriorate to the point of renewed legal action, courts are increasingly ordering ex-couples to work out their differences via technology. A new crop of online custody tools has been specifically designed to keep sniping parents at bay.[18]

Keeping Families Connected

Before the Internet, a dad who worked extensively overseas might see his children three to four times a year *if* he could afford to travel home. Today that same father can see and speak with loved ones daily via Skype and webcam, while emailing and texting photos and video as often as he wants throughout each day. In this way he can remain very much a part of their daily lives.

Consider Lawrence, forty-five, a geologist who is a technical consultant to oil companies all over the world. He lives in Minnesota but doesn't have an office there. Instead, he is assigned to work in one remote location or another, wherever his services are required. The assignment might consist of three months in Venezuela or four months in Asia. This "traveling dad" lifestyle is familiar to Lawrence because his own father had a very similar career. Unlike his father, however, Lawrence has a very close relationship with his wife and children because he has access to them 24/7 via online technology. Is this experience the same as a hug and kiss when Dad or Mom gets home from work? No. But consider Lawrence's view of his own father and childhood life, pre-Internet:

When I was a child I hardly knew my father, as he left home for work several times a year for many months at a time. In essence, my mom raised me in a single-parent home. My dad dutifully sent me a letter or postcard weekly, and my mom encouraged me to reply. Both of my parents sent pictures back and forth, keeping each other up-to-date on family activities and major events. But essentially, my dad was a stranger to me. It was only after my father retired that the two of us began to establish a meaningful relationship.

< 54 >

In contrast, Lawrence and his wife, Linda, are in constant contact, no matter where he is. They email and text during the day, and most evenings they have a date to talk online via webcam. On these little-to-no-cost live video chats the couple spends hours discussing how the day went, what each did, and any decisions that need to be made related to home and family. Lawrence was 3,000 miles away when his daughter took her first steps, yet he saw and encouraged it live on the computer. Now he helps his kids with homework, plays games with them online, tells them bedtime stories, and sings them softly to sleep even when thousands of miles away. Lawrence is an active participant in his family's life, and he and his wife consider themselves to be very close emotionally.

With the memory of his own childhood ever present, Lawrence makes every effort to be an active husband and father, despite the work-related physical distance from his family that he experiences much of the time. He surely misses the physical contact with Linda and his kids, but he also knows that they do not feel unsupported. At times, when family and friends are not around and when Lawrence and Linda are feeling particularly close, they remind themselves of their sexual relationship by describing in detail what they would like to do when they are next together in bed. This often ends in mutual masturbation via webcam, which both acknowledge is not their preferred sexual activity, but it does help them to feel connected to each other while keeping vital parts of their relationship alive and not "put on hold" until the next actual visit.

The families most commonly separated for long periods by work are those in the military. While old-fashioned snail-mail is still an option for these folks, especially when sending packages, the military now offers a wide variety of newer, more efficient forms of family communication.[19] For instance, you can send email to any soldier at his or her Army Knowledge Online (AKO) email address. Family members can also get their own AKO account, which allows them to instant message (IM) family members in Iraq, Afghanistan, and other venues. There are a number of such Internet cafes situated on U.S. bases in Iraq. In addition, secure video teleconferencing systems are provided at Family

< 55 >

Readiness Centers on U.S. posts. These allow soldiers to participate in real-time video chats with loved ones back home. The emotional and psychological benefits of soldiers being able to maintain contact with their families is now clearly recognized by the military, whose technical support specialists have set up numerous ways to use new communication technologies.

Filling a Much-Needed Gap

Twenty-five years ago, young lovers found it difficult to keep a relationship going if work or education sent them in different directions. Today's technologies have enabled many couples to stay in closer contact and thus make different decisions. A college student describes what long-distance love is like for his generation: "I've read that 90 percent of human communication is nonverbal. Skype captures that 90% on low-resolution video camera, compresses it, funnels it to another computer, and reproduces it on a screen anywhere in the world. Skype eliminates distance; that's why it works."[20] With email, chat, and Skype, couples don't have to end their relationship if one or the other gets a distant job. "High school couples no longer have to split up should one stay home or if they attend different colleges because couples can still spend practically every waking moment in virtual communication. The same goes for foreign-study and summer flings that carry on after lovers are once again separated by time and distance."[21]

Thanks to technology, today older people with changed personal or professional circumstances can more easily investigate new career, educational, and social options in the privacy of their own homes. They don't have to worry about appearing embarrassingly needy, lonely, or unwanted to the outside world. Also, people with more profound physical limitations can continue to work, learn, and interact with friends and family, again without having to leave home. And while some older people are still not yet comfortable with email and other forms of online communication, the scrapbooking aspects of Facebook are appealing. The immediate grandkid-interactivity offered by Skype and FaceTime are quickly decreasing the number of "old fogies" who would rather watch TV than engage with loved ones via modern technology.

< 56 >

Today, most people in the United States don't live in large families, nor do they live in extended family communities with relatives they've known well for all or even most of their lives. Few of us live at the same address for thirty years or more as did our parents. American cultural mobility has often resulted in a lack of community and reduced involvement in the church and social service clubs like the Lions, Moose, and Rotary. Whether by mere good fortune or as a medium whose popularity evolved partly out of our changing notions of family, home, and community, the Internet may have come along to fill a much-needed gap. And with it we now have robust diversity, cultural richness, and a plethora of previously unimaginable, evolving new ways to more fully engage with others.

As with all forms of human/social/technological change, these advances will be good for some and bad for others. Those who learn to effectively absorb information and use new technologies in healthy ways will flourish, and those who don't will likely feel increasingly disconnected from our technology driven world.

< 57 >

CHAPTER THREE

Parenting Healthy Children in the Digital Age

To watch a toddler actively engage digital technology
is to view human evolution in real time.
—Robert Weiss, LCSW (author)

The minds of infants and toddlers are wildly adaptive, absorbing and processing information at an almost unfathomable pace. At the same time that infants are learning to move their limbs, chew and swallow food, comprehend, mimic, and even speak, they are also developing abstract thoughts on at least a rudimentary level. Consider the young child whose parents hold a phone to his or her ear so the child can "talk to" Grandma. One might theorize that such a toddler thinks the nice lady with the purse full of sweets is somehow ensconced in Mommy's iPhone, but anyone who's ever looked into a child's eyes while this is going on can see this isn't the case. Young children may not completely understand the situation, but it's clear they somehow "get" that Grandma is someplace else and they're only hearing her voice through the device that's pressed against their ear. In other words, toddlers' brains accept and adapt to telephones (and most other technologies) with incredible and almost instantaneous ease.

Research indicates that even infants are capable of learning new technology and interacting with sophisticated mobile devices. Toy companies actually have researchers, known in the industry as "spelunkers," watch children play with various digital apps to learn what they are capable of at various ages. One Fisher-Price spelunker reports, "We see 6-month olds batting at the screen, 9-month olds swiping, and

< 59 >

12-month olds pointing out objects to see."[1] Another Fisher-Price spelunker observed an eighteen-month-old discovering the joys of Net-
flix—selecting a show to watch and even rewinding to replay a favorite
scene.[2] This child is doing this six months to a year before most kids can
speak full sentences! The company is now developing a stuffed monkey
with a place in its belly to position an iPhone (with a sturdy cover, of
course), allowing kids to more readily play with the hundreds of early
childhood learning apps already on the market.[3] Today's newborns are
literally being weaned on touch devices, adapting to their use nearly as
intuitively as they will reach up to be held when afraid.

Digital Darwinism?

Our astonishing ability as human beings to absorb, adapt, and learn
new ways of functioning throughout our life spans is known as *neuro-
plasticity* or *brain plasticity*. Scientifically speaking, plasticity is the innate
ability of the brain to change itself, its very "wiring," and to reorganize
according to our life experiences. This means that our brains are *not*
hardwired with fixed and immutable circuits that are unchanging from
early life onward. Rather, our brains can and do change over time—
most profoundly during infancy, childhood, and adolescence—but also,
albeit more slowly, right up to our last days of life.

This is not to say that our development is all nature over nurture.
As Lisa Eliot wrote in *Scientific American*, "Brain differences are indisputably biological, but they are not necessarily hardwired. The crucial,
often overlooked fact is that *experience itself changes the brain structure and
function*."[4] Eliot explains:

> Obviously, girls and boys are not identical at birth: genetic and
> hormonal differences must launch the male and female brain
> down different developmental pathways. But early experience,
> we now know, permanently alters the chemistry and function of
> genes inside cells, leading to significant effects on behavior....
> Most sex differences start out small—as mere biases in temper-
> ament and play style—but are amplified as children's pink- or
> blue-tinted brains meet our gender-infused culture, including

< 60 >

all the tea parties, wrestling matches, playground capers and cafeteria dramas that dominate boys' or girls' existence.[5]

In similar ways, digital technology is influencing the minds (via neural plasticity) of young people of both genders—especially those who use it from birth onward. The question, of course, is how will this tech-driven, neurobiological revolution affect us over the long haul? The answer is *we do not know.*

One thing that we do know for certain is that early, repeated engagement with digital technology will affect our species long term. It turns out that nearly all information we are exposed to in infancy and toddlerhood sticks with us. For instance, numerous studies show that what a child learned during the extreme (early) brain plasticity stage is never completely forgotten. One study showed that even though many infant/toddler adoptees and emigrants from non-English-speaking nations have no conscious memory of their native tongue, much of the often subtle linguistic information processed in the first months of life remains in the brain. For instance, English-speaking adults who were exposed to Hindi or Zulu as infants or toddlers but who have no conscious memory of the language as adults are nearly always able to learn (relearn?) the subtle sound contrasts inherent in these languages, whereas adults who weren't exposed to those languages early on typically cannot.[6] More simply: How many of us recall being toilet trained or learning to walk? Yet nearly all healthy adults retain these skills *without conscious memory* of when or how they were learned. In this way we can see that the brains of very young children absorb, process, and store almost unfathomable amounts of information—much of which can be accessed at virtually any point later in life if/when needed.

How Much Tech is Too Much Tech?

The answer to this is we simply do not know. However, there are varied opinions on this depending on who you ask. For example, when you bring your child to the pediatrician for a well-child visit, you may be greeted with a couple of new questions:

< 61 >

- How much recreational screen time does your child or teenager consume daily?
- Is there a television set or Internet-connected device in the child's bedroom?

The American Academy of Pediatrics (AAP) released a policy statement about Children, Adolescents, and the Media in October 2013 which encourages pediatricians to ask parents these two media questions at every well-child visit. The policy also included some guidelines for parents on how much "screen time" to allow their children:

- limit the total of entertainment screen time to less than 1 to 2 hours per day
- discourage screen media exposure for children less than 2 years of age
- keep the TV and Internet-connected devices out of the child's bedroom
- monitor what media children are using and accessing
- coview TV, movies, and videos with children and teenagers, and use this as a way of discussing important family issues
- model active parenting by establishing a family home use plan for all media
- establish reasonable but firm rules about cell phones, texting, Internet, and social media use[7]

The reality is we don't have any peer-reviewed research studies on the impact of interactive screen use for children under age 2. People are beginning to question what these AAP guidelines are based upon. Because there is no research available at this time to show the long-term impact of "screen time" on our children, expect guidelines from the AAP and other organizations to change frequently as we begin to learn more about the positive and negative impact of technology on our youth. Meanwhile, some parents are getting frustrated on whose advice to follow.

< 62 >

I wish I knew how much time is healthy for my kids to play with their PlayStations, Wii's, iPads, and computers versus putting that all down and just being a kid. Every parent I talk to has a different opinion, as do the kids' teachers, faculty, and counselors. No one seems to know exactly what is healthy for them now or in the days to come. I want to give my kids the best advantage to conquer the road ahead of them, and clearly much of that will involve mastering information technology and the virtual world. But at the same time, what do I say when my son would consistently prefer to play on his "pad" than simply go outside to play on a nice day? This is a kid who would rather "interact" with virtual lions and giraffes on a screen than spend an afternoon at the zoo. As a caring mother, how am I to know what's right?

Suzanne, mother to Charlie (age 5) and Miriam (age 2)

For some clues on how much tech is too much tech, let's return to the basic question of how early and persistent engagement with technology is affecting the brains, personalities, and lives of our children—not to mention the generations to come. And the answer is that it is far too early to know how this will play out, as we do not yet have the necessary amount of unbiased, broad-based, longitudinal, multi-generational, cross-cultural research to reach definitive conclusions. Our lack of solid research has not, however, prevented a wide array of speculation—*most of it sadly being negative conjecture by older (digital immigrant) professionals.* Unfortunately, these empathic, caring, well-educated individuals seem only able to view (and give opinions) on the intergenerational effects of technological change through a lens that is itself distorted by expertise gained through their own time, place, generation, relationship experiences, and culture. This type of retrospective analysis, even when well intentioned, can produce concerns based primarily on fear of the unknown, fear of change, and the very human belief that "the way we did it (whatever *it* may be), is the best way to do it."

One *New York Times* article describes the concerns of (digital immigrant) pediatrician Ari Brown. In the article, Brown states:

< 63 >

> Infants learn from real people and playing with real toys. They learn how to communicate, how to engage with others and how to problem solve using their five senses. While technology can offer a virtual way to learn some of these skills, [technology] will never replace the value of interacting with humans, or being able to manipulate and play with toys in one's hands.[8]

Another (digital immigrant) pediatrician voiced a similar concern to one of the authors of this book, recalling several occasions when parents in her office were so busy texting and reading their iPhones that they had minimal eye contact with their kids. When a child persisted in getting the parent's attention, the parent would quickly attend to the child's needs and then return to his or her iPhone. "Small kids learn to relate to others through eye contact," said the pediatrician. This doctor's fear is that these kids will find it difficult to interact with live people as they grow into adult life.

Dr. Sherry Turkle, another digital immigrant, echoes this sentiment in her book *Alone Together: Why We Expect More from Technology and Less from Each Other*. She discusses toys that blur the boundaries between the living and the mechanical such as the Furby (a small robotic hamster-like creature) and AIBO (a small robotic dog). Both toys were designed to be treated as pets rather than machines, and research shows children often feel as if these toys are alive and need love. A Furby even complains if it is handled inappropriately. A more recent robotic doll, My Real Baby, does not respond to pain because the manufacturer was worried that doing so might encourage some children to exhibit sadistic behavior. Instead of complaining when it is shaken, spanked, or otherwise handled in a way that would hurt a real child, it simply shuts down. In most other respects, the doll is relatively realistic. Turkle writes of these toys:

> If they can give the appearance of aliveness and yet not disappoint, relationship artifacts such as sociable robots open new possibilities for narcissistic experience.... Children need to be with other people to develop mutuality and empathy; interacting with a robot cannot teach these. Adults who have already

< 64 >

learned to deal … easily with others and who choose to "relax" with less demanding forms of social "life" are also at risk. But whether child or adult, we are vulnerable to simplicities that may diminish us.[9]

Kids, Tech, and Reality

We have already noted that even the most clever and insightful professionals are limited in their ability to interpret today's experiences of kids and tech because they see through the distorted filter of their own life and times. We also noted that behavioral science does not yet have enough clinical research to proffer broad-based, factual conclusions about how digital technology is affecting our young children. It is also worth noting that most pediatricians, child psychologists, and parenting specialists writing about this today are more likely to see and experience the more troubled and challenged kids in our culture. That is their job. Furthermore, these professionals' experience with a more challenged youth population strongly influences their views, opinions, perceptions, and writing. Healthy, well-adapted children are much less likely to be closely scrutinized by even the most engaged clinicians, as those kids are out in the world playing, making friends (virtual or IRL), and enjoying family life.

Moving away from the academics, clinical prognosticators, media soothsayers and pediatricians for a moment, let's look at the realities of parenting in today's world. One thing is abundantly clear: *parents worry*. As Suzanne, the mother of two young children, so clearly articulated, most parents today are asking themselves, *Am I doing the right thing by letting my kid play with an iPhone or iPad? How long should she be allowed to play with it? Is that silly game where my kid "bakes cookies" by swiping at the screen (mostly making a mess in the virtual kitchen) educational, or is this turning his brain to mush? Do Angry Birds evolve angry kids?* Meanwhile, as we worry our kids are screaming for technology. They want it like they want candy. Parents often find themselves in conflict—excited by the potential of digital tech no less, yet wary of a potential downside. Consider the words of Hanna Rosin in a recent article in the *Atlantic*:

< 65 >

On the one hand, parents want their children to swim expertly in the digital stream that they will have to navigate all their lives; on the other hand, they fear that too much digital media, too early, will sink them. Parents end up treating tablets like precision surgical instruments, gadgets that might perform miracles for their child's IQ and help him win some nifty robotics competition—but only if they are used just so. Otherwise, their child could end up one of those sad, pale creatures who can't make eye contact and has an avatar for a girlfriend.[10]

Parents + Kids + Tech = Anxiety

Parents are all over the map on this issue. Stuart and Diane, a highly tech-savvy couple with a five-year-old son, allow their child to play games and watch his favorite movies on Stuart's hand-me-down iPad pretty much whenever he wants. They don't worry if the games or films are educational, only that their son is engaged and having fun. Conversely, Jack and Polly, both computer programmers, have seven children ranging in age from two to fourteen. They don't allow their children to "play" on digital devices at all. They also limit television to two hours of educational programming per week. Who is right and who is wrong? In most families a happy medium of some sort is reached; kids can play only after homework and chores or only for an hour a day. Hanna Rosin, a mother of three, writes of her experience:

> My youngest child … was not yet 2 when the iPad was released. As soon as he got his hands on it, he located the Talking Baby Hippo app that one of my older children had downloaded. The little purple hippo repeats whatever you say in his own squeaky voice, and responds to other cues. My son said his name ("Giddy!"); Baby Hippo repeated it back. Gideon poked Baby Hippo; Baby Hippo laughed. Over and over, it was funny every time. Pretty soon he discovered other apps. Old MacDonald, by Duck Duck Moose, was a favorite. At first he would get frustrated trying to zoom between screens, or not knowing what to do when a message popped up. But after about two weeks, he figured all

< 66 >

that out. I must admit, it was eerie to see a child still in diapers so competent and intent…. By age 3, Gideon would go to preschool and tune in to what was cool in toddler world, then come home, locate the iPad, drop it in my lap, and ask for certain games by their approximate description: "Tea? Spill?" (That's Toca Tea Party.)[11]

Of course, Rosin worries about Gideon's development as would any good parent. What limits should she set for Gideon? She decided to try, for six months, the same approach Stuart and Diane took with their son: Let him play as much as he wants and see what happens. Rosin continues:

Gideon tested me the very first day. He saw the iPad in his space and asked if he could play. It was 8 a.m. and we had to get ready for school. I said yes. For 45 minutes he sat on a chair and played as I got him dressed, got his backpack ready, and failed to feed him breakfast. This was extremely annoying and obviously untenable. The week went on like this—Gideon grabbing the iPad for two-hour stretches, in the morning, after school, at bedtime. Then, after about 10 days, the iPad fell out of his rotation, just like every other toy does. He dropped it under the bed and never looked for it. It was completely forgotten for about six weeks. Now he picks it up every once in a while, but not all that often. He has just started learning letters in school, so he's back to playing LetterSchool. A few weeks ago his older brother played with him, helping him get all the way through the uppercase and then lowercase letters. It did not seem beyond the range of possibility that if Norman Rockwell were alive, he would paint the two curly-haired boys bent over the screen, one small finger guiding a smaller one across, down, and across again to make, in their triumphant finale, the small z.[12]

Both Stuart and Diane report a similar experience with their son. Stuart says,

< 67 >

I don't download every game he wants, but he gets a newish one every week or two. Usually he plays with it for a day or so, and then he gets tired of it. Either he'll go back to playing another game that he likes better, or he wants to do something outside, or he wants attention from Diane or me. He pretty much self-regulates all this stuff, except at bedtime. But that doesn't have anything to do with the iPad. He just doesn't want to go to bed.[13]

Lisa Guernsey laid out some potentially good rules of thumb in her book *Screen Time*.[14] Guernsey suggests parents think about the following:

- Is the content loaded onto this machine age-appropriate for my child?
- Is the amount of time they spend engaged with this technology a large or small part of my child's total social interaction?

She also notes that parents' attitudes toward digital technology will affect how the child feels about it. In other words, if a parent treats a tech object or experience with fear and trepidation, as something "bad" to be minimized or avoided, the child may become tech averse, which will not serve him or her well over time in an increasingly digital universe. Child experts have long understood that if we make a desirable object or fun experience seem "bad" to a child, while also making the child feel "wrong" for showing interest in it, that ultimately this stance tends to make the object both more enticing and more likely to be used "in secret." Therefore, parents who are open and inquisitive about their child's involvement with tech, while also setting clear and understandable (to the child) limits around its use, are more likely to achieve a healthy result than parents who grab the tech toy out of their child's hands while saying that using it too much will turn his or her brain into pea soup. For example, some parents not only provide their children with smartphones, but require them to sign contracts which set clear guidelines around acceptable use.

< 68 >

As noted, many well-meaning, highly educated older adult professionals have expressed reasonable but factually unsubstantiated concerns that the younger generation's intensive engagement with technology may create a generation of young adults who fail to develop empathy and are, as a whole, uncomfortable with live social interactions. So, is it likely that future generations will be more adept and at ease with technological exchanges than with live human interaction? Will they become, as some older people fear, "sad, pale creatures who can't make eye contact"? Maybe yes and maybe no, but the most likely answer is … some yes and some no and … we simply don't know. What we do know is that these twenty-first-century fears have evolved out of twentieth-century beliefs and experiences that often don't accurately reflect the realities of the world our children currently face.

What we can, however, state here unequivocally is that tech is here to stay. If you're a parent, it is better to be prepared and have a well-thought-out plan than to simply avoid the issue or take it on as it shows up. Our children of all ages are using digital technology whether we like it or not. Is it affecting them? Yes, absolutely. Are they developing and growing up differently as a result? Yes, without question. But the likely outcome of this reality is both far from understood and too early to evaluate.

Teens Are People Too (Sort of)

Adolescents by definition act more impulsively than adults and are less likely to consider the long-term consequences of their actions. As a result they are far more likely to engage in risky, impulsive behavior.[15] Although the bodies of sixteen- to eighteen-year-olds may appear near adult, their brains are far from it. As a result, when compared with adults, juveniles have higher rates of accidents, drug and alcohol use, suicide, unsafe sexual behavior, and criminal activity. Furthermore, risk taking is higher among adolescents than among younger children. And functional magnetic resonance imaging (fMRI) studies of the adolescent brain show why.

Thanks to fMRI scans, we now know that different parts of the brain mature at different rates. The most significant difference in mat-

< 69 >

uration rates occurs in the prefrontal cortex and the striatum. The striatum, which includes the nucleus accumbens—sometimes referred to as the brain's "pleasure center"—controls sensation seeking, enjoyment, and reward. This part of the brain matures rather quickly, with a major growth spurt in early adolescence. Conversely, the prefrontal cortex, which controls rational thought and decision making, matures more slowly. In short, the part of the brain that recklessly seeks to have a good time evolves much earlier than does the sensible part of the brain that causes us to think things through before we act. This explains why teenagers, despite their intellectual ability, are often annoyingly impulsive. In essence, the human brain is designed to encourage their irresponsible behavior. From an "intelligent evolutionary design" standpoint, taking risks while seeking rewards promotes learning, emotional growth, as well as the parallel potential for late teen pregnancy (which is highly desirable, if only from an evolutionary standpoint). And so our late teen years are a period of time in which risky, impulsive activities are more attractive than safe, deliberate behaviors.

The end result is that human adolescence—roughly ages fourteen to twenty-five—represents a period of imbalance between emotional reactivity and reward seeking versus intellectual decision making. For some (perhaps most) teenagers, the emotional lure of immediate pleasure is more powerful than rational thinking. Even so, adolescents are quite capable of making rational decisions. They understand the risks of the behaviors in which they engage. It's just that when they are exposed to attractive, potentially pleasurable stimuli (think sex, drugs, and rock n' roll), their striatum (the gas pedal) is getting a lot more pressure than their prefrontal cortex (the brakes).[16] Their choices tend to be skewed even further if the risk-taking, pleasure-seeking behavior is encouraged by their peers, as is nearly always the case when it comes to digital technology (Facebook, Instagram, Twitter, Tinder, video games, and texting).

Game Stop

One issue of particular concern today among many parents is video gaming. The United States is the largest gaming market in the world, with approximately 183 million active gamers (people who say they

< 70 >

play video, computer, or other online games "regularly"). On average, these users spend 13 hours per week gaming. Approximately 97 percent of kids (old enough to play video games, but under eighteen) are *gamers* and, if asked, most of them expect to be gamers their entire lives. Today a typical young person has spent about 10,000 hours playing video games by age twenty-one. That's something like five years of 40-hour work weeks. Even more staggering, it's more than double the amount of time the average college student spends earning a bachelor's degree (4,800 hours). "Extreme gamers," comprising 4 percent of the U.S. population, average an astonishing 48.5 hours per week.[17]

Now that's a whole lot of gaming, which may or may not be a bad thing depending on the individual person and their life circumstances. As Jane McGonigal writes in her book *Reality Is Broken: Why Games Make Us Better and How They Change the World*:

> The truth is this: in today's society, computer and video games are fulfilling genuine human needs that the real world is currently unable to satisfy. Games are providing rewards that reality is not. They are teaching and inspiring and engaging us in ways that reality is not. They are bringing us together in ways that reality is not.[18]

McGonigal may be right in her assessment. Even so, that doesn't diminish the fact that younger people today—particularly tweens and teens—spend an enormous percentage of time interacting with technology. Keep in mind that the gaming statistics cited above *are in addition to* the amount of time most kids spend on social media sites, video sites, music download sites, and just plain "communicating" with one another via chats, IMs, and texts. One well-researched study estimates that kids ages eight to eighteen spend 11.5 hours per day using technology (computers, television, mobile phones, and video games) with many of those hours spent engaged with two or more technologies simultaneously.[19] Since most kids are awake for only fifteen or sixteen hours per day, somewhere between 71 and 76 percent of their day is now digitally engaged and/or enhanced.

< 71 >

Raising Technological Junkies?

The question, of course, is how 11.5 digitally interactive hours per day will affect kids in both the short and long term. What is this doing to their brains' "gas pedals" and "brakes"? What is the difference in the development of these children compared with those who grew up spending their days engaged in "live" social activities like team sports, study groups, nature walks, social clubs, and "real-world" dating? Is it possible that we're raising a generation of technological junkies who will suffer withdrawal symptoms if and when they are separated from their smartphones, people who will put going online (for whatever purpose) ahead of all else in their lives in the same way that drug addicts put getting high at the top of their priority list? Or are we merely raising a generation more perfectly attuned to survival in the fast moving, multitasking, tech-connect world into which they were born? Again, only time will tell. And the answers, once we discover them, will not be the same for all kids as each of us adapts differently to various types of stimulation.

Technology and Learning

In addition to spending a lot of time gaming, young people are learning—both in and out of school—differently from the way their parents did. Author Don Tapscott wrote about this as part of a series in *Business Week*:

> The differences stem from their immersion in digital technology. By the time they're in their 20s, the Net Generation, as I call them, will have spent more than 30,000 hours on the Internet and playing video games. This is happening at a time when their brains are particularly sensitive to outside influences, and it has changed their mental reflexes and habits, the way they learn and absorb information.[20]

In the article, Tapscott mentions Joe O'Shea, at that time the student body president at Florida State University. O'Shea told Tapscott that, like many his age, he doesn't read books, that instead he goes to Google.

< 72 >

O'Shea is quoted as saying that books are "not a good use of my time, as I can get all the information I need faster through the Web." By the way, if you think O'Shea is lazy and just taking the easy way out, you're dead wrong. This is a young man who set up a medical clinic in New Orleans after Hurricane Katrina, became student body president at a major university, cofounded an international student exchange system similar to the Peace Corps, and earned a prestigious Rhodes scholarship—all by the age of twenty-two.

Tapscott writes:

[Digital natives] don't necessarily read from left to right, or from beginning to end. They're more sensitive to visual icons than older people are, and they absorb more information when it's presented with visual images than when it's offered in straight text. This may help them be better scanners, a useful skill when you're confronted with masses of online information.[21]

One might argue that in attempting to absorb and make meaning out of short bursts of information—often multiple bursts at the same time—digital natives are apt to make more mistakes. One might also argue that they are less likely than digital immigrants to fully comprehend any given topic, that their understanding will at best be superficial or insufficient. After all, if you're not reading a book cover to cover, you might not be exposed to the author's fully developed argument. If you've not learned "longhand division," but instead grew up with a calculator, then you might lack the fundamental skills needed to make a daily budget. Or so the arguments go. Yet we don't question our ability to turn on a light even if we don't understand the fundamentals of electric current, switches, and lightbulbs. And let's face it, how many of us would ever board an airplane if we first had to understand Bernoulli's principle (used to calculate the lift-force of an airplane wing)?

The truth is that every generation has its shortcuts to knowledge. Digital natives' Internet-enabled, bite-sized approach to education is merely the latest freshest form of learning, one which may just prove to be every bit as effective as digital immigrants' methodology of read-

< 73 >

ing books from start to finish. In fact, this "new" approach might be even more effective because, instead of relying on someone else's overall interpretation of the material, digital natives can grab what they perceive to be pertinent facts and interpret that information for themselves. In other words, this new methodology may actually be teaching young people to more fully *think for themselves*—a skill that traditional approaches to learning (rote memorization of facts being one example) often fails to cultivate.

Look Both Ways When Entering the Digital Highway

Although video games and new forms of learning do evoke parental concern, the greatest fear for most parents is their child's online safety (and, by extension, their child's real-world safety). This is a very legitimate concern. With the increasing sophistication of search engines, online research, and GPS apps, it is growing more difficult by the day to maintain one's personal privacy—especially for children who often don't understand the need to withhold information. Kids who share personal data via texts, Twitter, or in chats—even by simply naming their school, giving their full name, or mentioning a parent's employer—can unwittingly and unknowingly create real life risks where they can become prey for online predators.

Cyberbullying

Sadly, it's not just online predators and adult content that parents need to worry about. Cyberbullying—the deliberate, repeated, and hostile use of the Internet and related technologies to harm other people—is primarily perpetrated by and against children, probably because they are more vulnerable than adults to such behaviors. In one instance in 2010, a fifteen-year old Massachusetts girl, Phoebe Prince, hanged herself after being bullied and humiliated via text messages and on Facebook for nearly three months by multiple students at her high school. That same year, a student at Rutgers University set up a hidden webcam in his dorm room to spy on his eighteen-year-old roommate, Tyler Clementi. Unexpectedly, he captured his roommate engaged in a consensual sexual encounter with another man. He then sent out texts and

< 74 >

tweets encouraging his friends to view the recorded encounter online, where he had posted it. Three days later, Clementi jumped to his death from the George Washington Bridge in New York City. His roommate was arrested and served a mere twenty days in jail as a consequence of cyberbullying.

Phoebe Prince and Tyler Clementi are far from the only victims of cyberbullying. They are merely the most publicized of many suicides and other acts of emotional and physical self-harm that have resulted from this entirely new genre of personal persecution.

Fortunately, government agencies are beginning to take action against cyberbullying by providing useful direction and education to both parents and educators, and also by passing laws prohibiting such activity. The most prominent of these laws, the Protecting Children in the 21st Century Act, passed by the U.S. Congress in 2011, mandates that school districts update their policies to include education on cyberbullying. As a result, in places like Tucson, AZ, school districts are now educating students on appropriate versus inappropriate online behavior, including their social media interactions and posts. Equally important, middle schools and high schools are now beginning to offer technology workshops for parents. In many U.S. schools today, all K-12 principals and staff must now go through an annual training on bullying behaviors, including cyberbullying. In many states, electronic bullying and harassment are now viewed as serious harms, with potential consequences for the offending student ranging from a parent-administrator conference to detention or suspension. More severe cases are now routinely referred to legal authorities.

Sexting

Now that computers and smartphones have built-in digital cameras and webcams, it is incredibly easy for anyone to impulsively take a provocative snapshot of themselves and send it to another person. Once that image is sent, the person who sent it loses all control over it. The recipient may then choose to send it on to others or post it online for public viewing. Because of this, sexted images can now redefine what it means to have a "bad breakup," as resentful former boyfriends or girlfriends

< 75 >

can send and/or post an ex's nude photos pretty much anywhere, anytime without the sender's consent.

Of further concern is that when minors sext a photo, even to other teens, they are violating laws that prohibit the making and dissemination of child pornography. Numerous teens (typically fourteen to eighteen years old) have been arrested and charged with this offense, even when there was no malicious intent. For example, among an estimated 3,477 sexting cases that came under police scrutiny during 2008–2009, one-third were classified as "non-aggravated," meaning they were considered to be nothing more than adolescent experimentation. Nevertheless, 18 percent of these cases led to an arrest and formal charge. The remaining two-thirds of these incidents were considered "aggravated," meaning they involved additional criminal or abusive elements beyond just sending a sexual image. In about half of those cases an adult was involved, either as the recipient or as a solicitor of the image. In the remaining cases only teens were involved. The youth-only cases were considered "aggravated" only if they involved intent to harm (extortion, sexual abuse, or maliciousness) or were examples of "reckless misuse," such as when the photos were distributed without the knowledge of or against the will of the person in the image. In nearly all cases, the photos in question were both taken and distributed by smartphones. In one aggravated incident, a sixteen-year-old girl accidentally uploaded a nude photo of herself to a social networking site. Although she quickly deleted the image, another teen from her school had already seen and downloaded it. He then threatened to distribute it if she didn't send him more provocative pictures. When she refused, he forwarded the photo to about one hundred other people at their school. This boy was later arrested and charged with a felony, pled guilty, and was placed on probation.[22]

Although teen sexting has received a lot of media attention because of its shock value, it is actually rather uncommon. Only about 1 percent of youths aged ten through seventeen say they have knowingly created, sent, or appeared in sexually explicit imagery. Teens engaging in experimental sexting may or may not face arrest as a consequence. Nevertheless, for any teenage girl or boy, having your nude picture passed

< 76 >

around your school or posted online can be a far worse (and longer lasting) punishment than jail. Keep in mind that these images won't automatically disappear by the time the child hits college or starts looking for a job. They can live online indefinitely.

Online Porn

For kids in the pre-Internet era accessing pornography was not an easy task. Often a male teen or one of his friends had to locate and surreptitiously raid his dad's stash of *Playboy* magazines or videos, inherit some porn from an older brother, snatch a magazine from the local drug store, or find porn in a neighbor's trash can or a dumpster. And even when accessed, old school porn offered a limited number of images and experiences. What you bought, stole, or found was what you got—no more, no less.

Those sepia-toned analog days are long gone. In the digital age, endless amounts of both soft- and hardcore pornography are widely and instantly accessible to anyone who goes looking for it—and often to people who aren't looking for it. If a teenage boy (or girl) is curious about sex, all he or she needs to do is find a porn site, click a button that says "Yes I'm 18," and access is granted. There is no need for a driver's license to prove one's age, no need to borrow Mom or Dad's credit card, and no one looks at you "funny" when you go to pay. Pornography of every ilk, stripe, and style imaginable is now ubiquitous, accessible to everyone 24/7 from any smartphone, tablet, or laptop, and more often than not it's free.

Even kids who aren't seeking porn can be exposed to inappropriate imagery. Consider the following:

Randall, a divorced dad, spent Saturdays with his nine-year-old son, David. On a recent outing to the local zoo David borrowed his father's smartphone to take some pictures of a gorilla. Afterward, as David checked on his dad's phone to see how his pictures turned out, he inadvertently stumbled across a series of explicit nude images. Most of the images David saw were of naked women, but a few of them also included David's dad in

< 77 >

various stages of undress, arousal, and sexual activity. David said nothing at the time; he simply handed the camera back. When David got home, however, mom got the whole story.

Children's exposure to adult pornography, once only an occasional experience, is today extremely common. In a 2008 survey of 594 university students (median age nineteen years), 93 percent of the male students and 62 percent of the female students reported having seen hardcore online pornography prior to age eighteen. Typically, their first exposure occurred between ages fourteen and seventeen. Boys reported viewing pornography more frequently, while also viewing more varied images than did girls. Seeing the sexual imagery was reported as a positive experience for many of the adolescents, especially the boys (big surprise), 80 percent of whom stated it left them "feeling sexual excitement." In contrast, only 27 percent of the girls reported feeling "turned on" by the images. Some common negative reactions reported among both genders were embarrassment, shame, guilt, confusion, and feelings of inadequacy as they compared themselves to the online images naively viewed as accurate depictions of anatomy and healthy sexuality.[23] It is important to note that this study was conducted in 2008, before the current Internet/social media "porn explosion." More recent research suggests the average age of first exposure to Internet porn may now be as low as age eleven.[24]

Anticipating and coping with a child's unintentional exposure to pornography should now be a part of every parent's responsibility, as is preplanning a response to finding your teen intentionally viewing online porn, sexting to friends, or engaging in other digitally driven sexual activity. *In other words, parents today need to educate their children about healthy, intimate sexuality or their child's sexual education will occur primarily via Internet porn.*

Online Predators

Another serious risk to children is potential exposure to sexual predators through social media and other online connections. In 2000, Katherine Tarbox wrote a book describing her experience as a young teen who

< 78 >

barely escaped being raped after making such a connection. Tarbox connected with another kid in a young people's chat room and eventually agreed to meet her suitor in person. That "boy" turned out to be an adult predator. Her family, searching for her by checking her phone and computer, located her in this man's hotel room and rescued her moments before she was physically assaulted. Tarbox's experience was relatively uncommon only a dozen years ago. Today, however, the existence of countless virtual games and live social networks, most of them offering GPS applications, makes it quite simple for predators to lure or seek out unsuspecting children as victims.

GPS software combined with "friend finder" smartphone apps has created an obvious risk to youngsters that may mystify their less tech-savvy parents. And the potential for such abuse increases daily. Skout, for example, is a mobile phone app specifically designed for flirting with strangers. Most Skout users sign in through Facebook (which officially "forbids" members under age thirteen). In 2011, when Skout's staff determined that a large percentage of their members were age seventeen and under, they started a separate, more protected service for teens. Nonetheless, adults posing as teens were consistently found to be entering this new site with a focus on connecting with underage victims. In 2011, three children—ages twelve, thirteen, and fifteen—were raped by adults they met via this online app, each of whom had posed as a new teen friend. After learning of these crimes, Skout suspended its service for minors until more safety measures could be put in place.

Another popular website with teens is Chatroulette, which pairs strangers at random for online video chats. Many people also use it for sexual purposes. The website states that users must be at least eighteen years old, but how many adolescents have ever been stopped by that type of warning? On Chatroulette and similar sites, children are and will continue to be unwittingly "exposed" to online voyeurs and exhibitionists. Of note here is that exactly the same exhibitionistic masturbatory act that will get you swiftly arrested if done in your car on a school campus, in a mall parking lot, or at the beach is not at all illegal when done to unsuspecting adults or children online.

< 79 >

To Sum It Up

Older generations often fearfully label and negatively judge technological change (except the ones they grew up with). This is most likely based more on fear of swift cultural change than on facts. Oftentimes these changes are thought to be "the end of the world as we know it." But how many of these changes have actually brought humanity to a screeching halt, and how many have instead brought us into a far more articulate, advanced era? Consider how many of us today would quickly go into "withdrawal" if separated from our microwaves, automobiles, and indoor plumbing—all technologies initially decried as being "dangerous to our health," "the devil's tools for a lax society," and "symptomatic of a culture in ruin." Perhaps digital technology is not the great social evil that many may fear it to be but simply another turn of our evolutionary wheel.

Nevertheless, concerns about the effects of childhood exposure to adult sexual imagery or inappropriate online contact are legitimate. Will kids exposed to these things develop problems with intimacy and relationships later in life? To date, we simply don't know. In the absence of detailed long-term research, the best we can conclude is that healthy children with good social skills and self-esteem may have a passing fascination with porn and other forms of online sexuality if exposed to these things in their teen years, but ultimately they will find their online sexual experience to be unsatisfyingly two-dimensional.

Conversely, at-risk children, those who carry histories of trauma, emotional neglect, and social inhibitions, may well be at long-term risk from early exposure to pornography, excessive online gaming, and reduced "live" social engagement. Now as it has always been, these children are likely to be more impulsive, vulnerable, and needful, so for them being exposed to a dangerous world (online) poses greater risks for harm.

< 80 >

CHAPTER FOUR

Tech, Sex, and Love

*We're born, we live for a brief instant, and we die. It's been happening
for a long time. Technology is not changing it much—if at all.*
—*Steve Jobs*

As author John Gray succinctly depicts in his book, *Men Are from Mars,
Women Are from Venus*, there are significant differences in the ways many
men and women typically think, act, and react, with many of these dis-
similarities related to our differing neurobiology. For starters, men tend
to be more analytical. When a partner or friend complains of a dilemma,
a man is most likely to respond with a proposed solution to the problem.
Women in similar situations tend to focus less on finding an immediate
"answer" and more on empathizing with the person suffering, holding off on offering suggestions and solutions until that person's feelings
have been discussed and worked through. In essence, women tend to
view problems more holistically, whereas men tend to be laser-focused
on the problem itself, sometimes even viewing the person's emotions
and feelings as potential roadblocks to a fast solution.

These and other basic gender differences are apparent in nearly every facet of modern life, including the utilization of digital technology.
Although men and women now use the Internet in equal numbers, they
often do so in very different ways. Men are more likely to engage in
video gaming, pornography, role-playing games, and other entertain-
ment-related activities, whereas women are more likely to go online for
work, education, shopping, communication, and to obtain personal information about other people. Women are also more likely than men to

< 81 >

use social media, which appears to mirror their innate desire for communication, connection, and interaction. From a sex and intimacy standpoint, current research indicates that men tend to favor more visually driven experiences like viewing porn and being sexual via webcam, and women tend to seek out online relational activities (chatting and instant messaging).[1]

One recent study found that women are more likely than men to use technology not only to find and secure a relationship, but also to minimize third-party threats to that relationship by announcing their relationship status on social media—for instance, making their dating "Facebook Official" (FBO). In other words, a woman will change her Facebook status from "single" to "in a relationship," and then typically post about who she is dating, how long they've been going out, how serious it is, and so on.[2] This behavior is particularly true of younger female digital natives. The study suggests that women go FBO to ward off other women, whereas men oftentimes don't go FBO because of their greater hereditary/biological/sociocultural interest in pursuing multiple partners. In essence, women use the Internet to "double down" on relationships (to find them and to protect them) whereas men are much more likely to go online purely for sexual gratification. This does not, however, mean that men do not seek lasting relationships using digital technology, merely that they are less likely to do so than women.

Love and Tech Are Many-Splendored Things

Whatever the technology, humans inevitably seem to adapt it and use it to find and develop romantic relationships. The Internet is no exception. As older readers are certainly aware, chat rooms were the first online venues for widespread interpersonal connection. The 1998 hit movie *You've Got Mail* provides a wonderful snapshot of this phenomenon. In the film, Tom Hanks portrays Joe, who owns a chain of bookstores, and Meg Ryan portrays Kathleen, who owns an independent bookstore that is slowly going under thanks to Joe's nearby, recently opened megastore. Hoping to save her business, Kathleen uses chat rooms to organize a boycott of her much larger competitor. Meanwhile, using the screen name "Shopgirl," she develops a romantic online relationship

< 82 >

with "NY152," who turns out to be Joe. While much of the movie's box office success was due to the chemistry and popularity of its two stars, the timely dramatization of their online interactions was equally appealing, as millions of people were also hitting the then wildly popular online chat scene, experiencing (or hoping to experience) similar connection and fulfillment.

Of course, text-driven chat rooms had a major shortcoming in that you never really knew who you were actually chatting with. That buxom blond that turned you on like crazy might actually have been an 85-year old coot named Herman, a circus freak, or even your cousin Betty. And if the other person sent you a personal photo (or used one in conjunction with his or her screen-name), there was no way to know if it was actually that person's photo or someone else's. And if it was their photo, there was no way to know how recent or accurate it was. Many people who chose to meet in real life after a brief or even a lengthy online chat were seriously disappointed by the person who actually showed up. To address this deficiency, most current-day chat rooms and instant messaging sites are now webcam enabled, allowing for live, face-to-face (or at least cam-to-cam) interaction, making it much easier to know if you are physically attracted to the person with whom you're chatting.

Online chat is just part of the modern dating and mating process. These days, millions of people have online personal ads, known as "profiles," on dating sites and phone apps, complete with photos and sometimes even videos. Some digital dating services are clearly more relationship-oriented while others are overtly sexual, with nearly all services containing a mix of people seeking long-term intimacy and people interested in a shorter-term situation. Many dating websites and apps cater to a specific segment of the population, such as gay (Adam4Adam. com), lesbian (PinkCupid.com), Jewish (JDate.com), Christian (ChristianMingle.com), or African American (BlackPeopleMeet.com). Others cater to a broad swath (eHarmony.com, Match.com). Dating sites are popular among baby boomers, who consider the chance to meet people online a welcome alternative to blind dates, church socials, and singles bars. And online dating is more efficient for busy folks with kids and jobs. Melissa, a fifty-year-old divorced mother, is an excellent example:

< 83 >

My first husband and I married right out of college—too young, and before either of us really understood what being married was all about. We toughed it out for as long as we could, but shortly after our third child was born—I was 38 when that happened—we decided to call it quits. At first I was okay with being a single working mother of three very active kids. That alone took up all my time. But then the kids hit their teens and they wanted some space. Suddenly I had free-time and I wasn't sure what to do with it. One of my friends suggested I go online and set up a dating profile. I did that, and I was totally honest— single mother of three hoping to meet someone fun and interesting who likes kids. I still haven't met Mr. Right, but I've had a lot of fun dating, just like I did in high school and college. It's been a good experience, and I'm glad I took the chance.

Live Versus Virtual

With all this online interaction, one wonders: Are virtual exchanges as healthy and rewarding as in-person connections? Generally speaking, healthy, intimate, trusting relationships require the following:

- **Respect:** shown by taking an active interest in others, having empathy for their challenges, and championing their successes
- **Support:** given by lending a helping hand when needed, providing advice when asked, and by genuine acts of kindness and acknowledgment
- **Quality time:** exhibited by communicating and interacting, learning about each other and playing together in ways that lead to a lasting connection
- **Validation:** given by valuing who another person is, by recognizing what he or she brings to the table, and by championing all that is special and unique about that person
- **Affection:** displayed through physical acts such as hugging, kissing, and embracing, and also by simpler

< 84 >

acts such as placing a hand on someone's shoulder as a display of understanding or solidarity

- **Vulnerability:** expressed by being genuine and open, allowing potential friends and loved ones to know you fully, and tolerating healthy fears of rejection, criticism, and abandonment
- **Trust:** earned over time via reliability, consistency, honesty, and commitment

In at least a few of these areas, digital exchanges come up short. Clearly, there is no virtual equivalent to the warmth of a supportive touch, hug, or kiss. At least not yet. Nevertheless, digital communication does in many ways enhance our ability to be "in touch" and to engage in at least some aspects of healthy relationship development. Certainly respect, support, and validation can be given over the Internet, vulnerability can be shown, and trust can be earned.

Unsurprisingly, a person's views on this subject often vary by age and upbringing, with digital natives typically displaying more ability and willingness than older generations to develop open, connected online relationships. In other words, young people are more likely than older people to accept and embrace the "reality" of a technological universe and the relationships formed and/or advanced therein.

Research on this topic actually skews in favor of digital natives' view of technology—that digital relationships really can be just as good as in-the-flesh relationships (or darn close, anyway). In fact, numerous studies demonstrate that communication via social networking sites, IMs, and texts can propel relationships forward, speeding up the "getting to know you" process by lowering inhibitions and allowing potential partners to be more genuine with each other, more quickly. A recent (non-scientific) survey jointly conducted by and published in both *Shape* and *Men's Fitness* magazines bears this out.[3] Eighty percent of the women surveyed said the Internet makes it easier to stay connected and therefore can lead to sex more quickly. Fifty-eight percent of men said digital flirting helps them get closer to women sooner. The study also found that texting today is the number one method for lovers to stay in

< 85 >

touch. Men said they text their intimate partners 39 percent more often than calling, and women said they text 150 percent more often.

It is certainly possible that such online interactions are fostering a "faux intimacy" among some couples. However, it is equally possible that this intimacy isn't faux at all, and the connections that some people experience through digital interactions are as real and meaningful as in-vivo flirting and dating—particularly in the early stages of a relationship. So while older generations are likely to yearn for the familiar face-to-face intimate exchanges they best understand and are comfortable with, digital natives may well consider a racy text message every bit as enticing as a wink and a smile from someone in the same room. In fact, a recent University of Michigan survey of 3,500 young adults (ages 18 to 24) found that for digital natives texting and sexting are simply "another way of flirting."[4]

Old Fogey Syndrome

Despite the increasing evidence that digital interactivity in healthy people enhances rather than detracts from their real-life experiences, many leading authors, clinicians, and sociologists (most often older digital immigrants) are less than sold on this idea. For example, in a recent ABC News article Dr. Dorree Lynn, a psychologist and the author of *Sex for Grownups*, writes, "It's easier to hop into bed than have a relationship. It's all a function of the fast-paced world we live in, where communication skills, genuine communication skills, which means face-to-face communication, are quickly going by the wayside."[5] Lynn strongly asserts that digital communication creates the type of faux intimacy mentioned above and that it does not teach people how to develop genuine relationships. "You let your fingers do the walking, and you can forget that you need to do the talking."[6]

The popular (anonymously written) blog *The Married Chick* espoused a similar sentiment in response to research on the increasing propensity of women to say "I love you" for the first time via text message:

When I read about this study, I wasn't surprised at all. But as a true romantic (not a hopeless one; a hopeful one!), I was sad-

< 86 >

dened. Mainly because I know that digital communication is well on its way toward replacing genuine, heart-thumping, palm-sweating human love interaction. I can remember long phone calls with my high school boyfriend. I lived for nights when I'd stay up past midnight, chatting with him about everything under the sun, hanging onto his every word. My kids will probably live this experience via IMs and text messages, typed at about 200 wpm! What's the heart-thumping, adrenaline-pumping pleasure in that? I can see setting up plans or sharing gossip via text, but saying "I love you?" It can't possibly have the same impact when you're reading it for the first time on your PDA (pun intended).[7]

What The Married Chick is really lamenting is the new generation gap. As Paul Lynde sang in the classic 1960s (baby boomer) Broadway-musical-turned-Hollywood-film, *Bye Bye Birdie*: "Kids! Why can't they be like we were, perfect in every way? What's the matter with kids to-daaaaaay?"[8] In truth, nothing at all is the matter with kids today. They're just digital natives, completely at home with the reality of intimate interactions that their parents and grandparents can't quite fathom having grown up in a very different world.

Tech-Sexy

Sometimes people aren't looking online for intimacy or romance at all. Instead, they're seeking to get aroused for a solo sexual encounter or to find anonymous, casual, or paid-for sexual partners. And there are many digital ways to achieve this. Among the most common is sexting, which allows people to be sexual with others regardless of where they are. The cameras (still and video) built into smartphones actually make this incredibly easy. All you have to do is snap a photo or shoot a quick video of your smiling face (or exposed body parts), pull up your intended's phone number, and hit "send." Voilà: instant, personalized pornography. And you can save those photos and videos for later sexts, making it possible to chat, flirt, exhibit yourself naked, and make a sex date—all while (in real time) you're at work, sitting on a park bench, or

< 87 >

dining in a crowded restaurant. For some, sexting is an exciting way to advance a budding relationship. Roger and Rene, who met through an online dating site, used sexting as a way to flirt and sexually connect long-distance. Rene writes:

> When we met, I was in Milwaukee and Roger was in Los Angeles. Initially, we communicated mostly using instant messaging on the dating service we both belonged to. Before long we were texting, too. After a couple of months, we started to feel like what was happening between us was something that might be more than just friendship, and we wondered if we might be sexually compatible. I decided to push the envelope one day and I sent him a sext—nothing too explicit, but still sexy (I hoped). That pushed our relationship forward enough that we decided to meet in person, and we're both glad that we did. After we'd known each other for a year, I quit my job in Wisconsin and moved to California. We've been together ever since.

At times sexting is used in conjunction with "adult friend finder" smartphone apps, which are much more about hooking up for casual or anonymous sex than actually making friends. Apps such as Grindr (for gay men), PinkCupid (for lesbians), Ashley Madison (for married people), and Skout, Blendr, Bang with Friends, and Tinder (for straight men and women) make casual encounters easier than ever. Traditional websites can also be used for this purpose, but mobile apps tend to be more effective, as apps are typically geared toward quick and dirty meetings that take place *right now* while websites are usually more focused on future hookups and longer-term relationships. Hookup apps are most popular with college students and young professionals who don't have the time (or desire) for a serious relationship. Megan, a medical student who uses both Skout and Tinder, says:

> Sometimes I take a night off from studying and hit a club with friends. When I was out a couple of months ago, I turned on Tinder and this guy David texted me right away. It turns out he

< 88 >

was in a club across the street, so I said if he came over to where I was I'd buy him a drink. Five minutes later, he was standing there in front of me. He's a professional ballet dancer. How sexy is that? And the great part is he wasn't looking for a relationship either. Our schedules are both too crazy for that. But we hooked up that night, and we've hooked up a few times since, totally without strings.

Dating and hookup websites and apps are also used by some people as a way to find escorts and "erotic services." Usually, if you find yourself chatting with someone on one of these sites or apps and that person tells you he or she is "working," it means he or she is willing to perform sexual acts in exchange for money or sometimes drugs. Yes, it's entirely possible that the person who professes to be working is simply chatting with you while taking a quick break from his or her desk at Morgan Stanley, but it's much more likely you're interacting with a prostitute.

Digital technology is also incredibly useful for people whose "love maps" (sexual arousal templates) are atypical. Prior to the Internet, men and women with sexual fetishes such as BDSM, cross-dressing, leather, feet, and the like, often led nonexistent, secretive, or unsatisfying sexual lives. Often these people felt isolated and alone, as if they were the only person with their particular sexual interest. Nowadays, however, it is very easy for like-minded individuals to find one another online. Consider the tale of Charlie, a gay "chubby chaser":

I always had a thing for big guys, right from the start. In school, we had this science teacher and he was a very big guy. I mean huge! And I had such a crush on him. To me, fat guys are sexy, and the bigger the better. For a long time, though, I felt like a freak because gay culture told me that I was supposed to be attracted to the guys in tight jeans and muscle shirts—not the ones in caftans! I felt totally out of place, and I learned that the obese guys who turned me on felt the same way. In fact, a lot of the guys I was attracted to told me that most evenings and weekends they just stayed at home, hiding, with no way

< 89 >

for someone like me to meet them. But that was then. Today, thanks to the Internet, I can find friends and partners all over the world. It doesn't matter where I live or who I know, I can go online and feel part-of, not alone, and not a freak. Nowadays I'm just another guy with "special needs," if you will.

In today's world virtually any fetish can now be discussed and experienced (both vicariously and in real life) via the Internet. For starters, online pornography has managed to eroticize nearly everything. More importantly, there are support groups that allow individuals with specific fetishes to meet, interact, and share practices. Shame is reduced and love of whatever it is that feels right can bloom.

And speaking of porn, it's no secret that the digital universe is practically overflowing with it. The days when copies of *Playboy, Hustler,* and other adult magazines were situated above the local convenience store counter, carefully out of reach of underage buyers, are long gone. Nowadays laptops and smartphones provide digital pornography of every ilk imaginable to anyone who's interested, regardless of age or location. Whatever it is that a person is into is readily available in virtually unlimited quantities—easily, instantly, and anonymously downloaded.

Increasingly often, online porn is free, in part because much of it is now produced by consumers (amateurs). Apparently a lot of people are quite exhibitionistic, willing to post nude images and/or videos of themselves engaged in sexual acts. Additionally, unscrupulous chat partners will sometimes post a sexted picture or record and post a cam-to-cam session where the other person is stripping, masturbating, or otherwise being sexual. As many have discovered, any online sexual interaction, including those that occur via smartphone, can easily end up on the Internet, available for public consumption, even though the "star" never intended for that to happen. And posting such files without permission is not even illegal!

Relatively recently, a new and evolving porn venue has cropped up: social media sites, especially Facebook and Instagram. Consider that approximately 250 million photos are uploaded to Facebook every day.[9] Most of these photos are personal snapshots. Nudity is not encouraged,

< 90 >

but it's not exactly discouraged, either, and it is available to those who seek it. So social media sites have become a new (and socially acceptable) place to peruse intimate photos, gain personal information, seek out hot chats, and hook up for virtual or in-person sexual encounters.

Men and Porn

In their recent TED Talk[10] turned eBook, *The Demise of Guys*, Philip G. Zimbardo and Nikita Duncan speak of the "technology enchantment" they believe is adversely affecting some young men in today's America. "From the earliest ages, guys are seduced into excessive and mostly isolated viewing and involvement with texting, tweeting, blogging, online chatting, emailing, and watching sports on TV or laptops. Most of all, though, they're burying themselves in video games and … online pornography."[11]

Aware of this, many parents worry that their sons are not learning what it takes to evolve healthy romantic and sexual partnerships. The fear is that young males may be using the non-intimate "intimacy" portrayed online as a model for their real-life relationships. And this may be a legitimate concern, as most Internet porn has no storyline, no emotional connection, and no buildup to the sexual performance. There is no talking, no seducing, no romancing, and no tenderness. Oftentimes kissing and foreplay are totally absent. Instead there is only an unending stream of idealized body parts and sexual acts. Zimbardo and Duncan assert that because of this, boys' brains are being rewired "to demand change, novelty, excitement and constant stimulation…. That means they are becoming totally out of sync … in romantic relationships, which tend to build gradually and which require interaction, sharing, developing trust, and suppression of lust at least until 'the time is right.'"[12]

Research does show that in addition to possibly being "out of sync" with potential partners, some young men are actually *losing interest in partner-sexuality altogether*. According to a 2012 *Japan Times* article examining the results of two 1,500-person surveys on male-female relationships—one survey conducted in 2008, the other in 2010—this issue may be more prevalent than one might initially expect. The 2010 study found

< 91 >

that 36.1 percent of males ages 16 to 19 had no interest in or an outright aversion to sex with another person. This figure was more than double that of the 2008 survey (17.5 percent). For males ages 20 to 24 the percentage increase was similar, up from 11.8 percent in 2008 to 21.5 percent in 2010.[13] Notice that this rising disinterest coincides directly with the no cost, amateur tech-connect porn boom, which took off around 2008. According to the article, "One young man said he has a sex drive but that having sex with [a real person] is 'just too much of a bother.' Others claim that they prefer girls as anime [animated] characters or as virtual dolls rather than the real thing…. Others explain that watching too much sex on Internet sites has left them with a bad taste in their mouth for human sexual contact. Many admit to extremely frequent masturbation with porn, thereby satisfying all their sexual needs themselves."[14]

Thanks to online porn, the "new reality" for at least some young men is that they appear less motivated than their predecessors to seek traditional forms of intimacy. "These guys aren't interested in maintaining long-term romantic relationships, marriage, fatherhood and being the head of their own family," Zimbardo and Duncan write. "Many have come to prefer the company of men over women, and they live to escape the so-called real world and readily slip into alternative worlds for stimulation. More and more they're living in other worlds that exclude girls—or any direct social interaction, for that matter."[15]

It is clear that the relationships and sexual behaviors of many of today's young males are not the same as the relationships and sexual behaviors of their fathers and grandfathers. This is true even when pornography is not involved, because, no matter what, digital natives spend a great deal of their lives online. As this occurs, many of the traditional rituals and practices of sex and romance occur digitally rather than in-person, as in the past. And online experiences are just plain different. For starters, they provide a fairly consistent guarantee of intensity and distraction. They also offer more control over how one is perceived, along with a lower risk of rejection. So if and when a young man whose development has been profoundly shaped by the use of digital media decides that he wants a "real" relationship, he may well find that he lacks the social skills required to make that happen. Some young

< 92 >

males may have lifelong struggles with physical and emotional intimacy, unable to successfully negotiate in-the-flesh flirtation, foreplay, dating, and long-term intimacy. That said, most young men will successfully adapt to new and evolving technologies, learning to incorporate them into their existence in healthy, life-enhancing ways. As to the men who do not adapt—those whom Zimbardo and Duncan and the study from Japan discuss—one potential outcome is that they may simply not mate and reproduce. This may well be a form of techno-evoked natural selection affecting our very evolution as a species.

Women and Porn

Researchers have long-known that male and female sexual arousal patterns are different. Men are most typically visually oriented, whereas women tend to be more interested in and turned on by relationship oriented sexuality. In recent years pornographers have become increasingly aware of these differences, generating new forms of "relationship-focused" erotic material designed to appeal to women. The most notably successful example of this is British writer E. L. James's bestselling trilogy of novels begun with *Fifty Shades of Grey*.

In most respects, the *Fifty Shades* books, along with a recent plethora of knockoffs (our society is nothing if not unoriginal), mirror the general reality of how men and women think about and experience sex. In fact, both reader reviews and anecdotal evidence suggest the vast majority of *Fifty Shades'* mostly female followers are entranced not so much by the books' graphic depictions of bondage and sexual domination, but by the development of the emotional relationship between the books' main characters, Anastasia and Christian, particularly Christian's eventual transition from cold, unemotional "master" to caring lover and concerned husband. A similar phenomenon, aimed at a younger female demographic, is the equally successful *Twilight* book/film series, with its exploration of young, beautifully sculpted, emotionally flawed male figures—presented here as vampires and werewolves—struggling with their desire to love and/or possess a beautiful young girl.

Of course, "mommy porn" (as *Fifty Shades* and the like have been dubbed) doesn't do it for all women. There are many healthy women

< 93 >

who enjoy highly objectified hardcore pornography just as much as men do. These women are perfectly comfortable viewing men (or women) in terms of their body parts. Basically, these women identify more with traditional male sexual stereotypes than traditional female sexual stereotypes.[16] Consider Anita, a 29-year-old woman who enjoys hardcore pornography, including imagery depicting BDSM:

> There are plenty of women out there, including myself, who are aroused visually in the way that men are, and we have some sexual and emotional characteristics that more closely follow the typical male pattern. For instance, I don't have sex to appease the man in my life or to get his love. I have sex for the rush of orgasm…. The fact that I get a bigger rush from sado-masochistic imagery than from vanilla porn is just part of the deal for me.

Studies show that Anita is far from alone, as a rapidly increasing number of women are accessing online pornography. In fact, today a third of all Internet porn viewers are women,[17] up from 14 percent in 2003.[18] So it seems that females in particular are taking advantage of the Internet's easy and anonymous access to porn, which allows them to enjoy potentially culturally shaming material in the privacy of their own home or on a portable device when alone.

Unsurprisingly, studies show that the women who use pornography are typically younger than those who prefer chat rooms and other "relational" activities. In other words, most active female porn users today are digital natives. According to one researcher, a possible explanation is that the younger generation is more accustomed to the huge quantity of visual stimuli that is now available.[19] Whatever the reason, women's increasing interest is porn is opening up a very healthy dialogue about female sexuality, not just in the therapeutic community and among gal-pals on their coffee breaks, but between women and their significant others. The simple truth is healthy women are profoundly sexual creatures—as much as men, albeit in different ways—and when women can more readily view or read about and then express their sexual thoughts

< 94 >

and desires to their partners it not only spices up their sex lives, it also helps to build and enhance relationship trust and emotional intimacy.

Is there a downside? An issue does arise for women who abuse sexual and romantic fantasy as a way to escape reality and avoid emotional challenges or those with underlying psychological issues like anxiety, depression, and childhood trauma. For these women, relying on the intensity of fantasy-based dissociation can become a "drug of choice," used much like alcohol or other drugs as a way to self-regulate uncomfortable emotions and tolerate life stressors. This behavior can, for some, escalate to the level of sexual/romantic addiction, resulting in serious negative life consequences. In this crucial way mommy porn presents the same concerns for psychologically vulnerable women as does hardcore, image-based pornography for emotionally challenged men.

Couples and Porn

Anecdotal evidence has long suggested that a heterosexual man's porn use can adversely affect the self-esteem of his girlfriend or wife, and a recent study supports this idea, finding that women whose romantic partners look at pornography frequently (in the female partner's estimation) are less happy in their relationships than women in relationships with men who either infrequently use porn or don't use it at all (to the woman's knowledge).[20] Essentially, the study concluded that as a boyfriend's or husband's porn use increased, the woman's self-esteem and relationship happiness decreased.

The most common complaint by women whose partners frequently used porn was that they felt as if they couldn't measure up to the images their partner was viewing online. Unfortunately, the study did not attempt to find out if the male's porn use caused the female's self-esteem to drop, or if women who already had low self-esteem were picking and sticking with "less available" partners (men with a pre-existing relationship to porn). Obviously more research is needed, but it is clear that the repeated use of porn by men in otherwise committed heterosexual relationships can and often does adversely affect their partners.

The reverse pattern does not seem to hold. Women may enjoy porn without upsetting their male partners. Sex therapist Ian Kerner writes:

< 95 >

In my experience, women tend to worry a lot more about their man's porn habits and what it means to their relationship, whereas many of the men I've spoken with tend to be intrigued by the idea of women and porn—especially since women are much more likely to enjoy porn that does not directly reflect their sexual orientation…. Who knows, perhaps the enormous variety of material offered by the Internet will end up playing more to the spectrum of female desire than male desire in the long run?[21]

Kerner also says that in the digital age he's seeing more couples who are enjoying porn together, often with the female taking the lead in choosing the material, and more women using porn to enjoy sexuality on their own (as most men do).[22]

Studies also show that a man's porn use can affect his ability to perform sexually. An increasingly well-documented cause of sexual dysfunction (both erectile dysfunction and delayed ejaculation) is related to "over-involvement with pornography" and use of masturbation as a primary sexual outlet. As psychiatrist Norman Doidge writes in his book, *The Brain That Changes Itself*:

[Porn abusers] reported increasing difficulty in being turned on by their actual (live) sexual partners, spouses or girlfriends, though they still consider them objectively attractive. When asked if this phenomenon had any relationship to viewing pornography, they answered that porn initially helped them get more excited during sex, but over time it seemed to have the opposite effect.[23]

Therefore, growing numbers of men may be suffering from sexual dysfunction that is directly related to their use of online pornography. And keep in mind the fact that heterosexual male sexual dysfunction affects women just as much as men. After all, if your man can't get it up, keep it up, or reach orgasm, then your sexual pleasure is likely to be diminished.

< 96 >

Interestingly, this problem is not simply due to the frequency of masturbation and orgasm outside a primary relationship. In reality the problem is increasingly related to the fact that when a man spends 75 percent or more of his sexual life masturbating to porn—endless images of young, exciting, constantly changing partners and sexual experiences—he is, over time, likely to find his longer-term real-world partner less stimulating than the new and exciting material in his head. In other words, for some couples the digital porn explosion is causing *an emotional disconnect that is manifesting physically as sexual dysfunction*. And no amount of Viagra or Cialis can "fix" this emotional issue.

Sexnology

The idea of "virtual sex" has long been a staple of science fiction. A very funny cinematic example (well-known to most baby boomers) occurs in the 1973 Woody Allen movie *Sleeper*, a comedy about life in the distant future. Among the movie's great fantasy inventions is the "orgasmatron," a contraption resembling a phone booth that causes users to experience orgasms through brain stimulation. Woody Allen actually confirmed the scientific feasibility of the orgasmatron prior to making the movie, so it's not surprising to learn about the existence of a real orgasmatron (discovered serendipitously in trials for a potential spinal cord stimulator). That device apparently works rather well, but it is costly and it requires the surgical insertion of electrodes near the spine. Needless to say, it is not widely used for pleasure.

There are, however, numerous less intrusive and more affordable "sexnologies" that can erotically simulate and stimulate. For instance, RealTouch has created a "teledildonic" male masturbation device that synchronizes in real time with whatever online porn is being viewed. Working in tandem with the activities taking place onscreen, the device warms itself up, lubricates, pulses, and grips. The process can also be engaged in with a live person—a loved one, a webcam performer, even a random stranger—who at their end stimulates a sensor-covered rod that transmits live signals across the digital universe to the receiving RealTouch device. In other words, people can now both give and receive virtual, electronically transmitted masturbation and oral sex. Fundawear

< 97 >

(smartphone activated underwear) operates on a similar principle—a swipe of the app at one end translates into pleasure at the other. In addition to the RealTouch device and Fundawear, more rudimentary toys that have been around for years are getting new features. For instance, inventors are reportedly working to create an iPad equipped with a Fleshlight holding case—placed strategically underneath the pad so users can "get off" hands-free while watching porn. (The Fleshlight, marketed as the "#1 selling male sex toy," mimics the sensation of a mouth, vulva, or anus using "real feel superskin.") For women there are similar virtual vibrators.

The future is equally engaging and curious in the realm of virtual-world sex, where users create customized fantasy avatars (animated versions of themselves), which they then use to participate in interactive online sexcapades. Many of these "worlds" cater to heterosexual males, but there are also games for straight women, gay men, lesbians, and people with fetishes. Some sites allow users to essentially produce their own porn—erotic scenarios, camera angles, musical scores, oversized body parts, etc.

Another evolving technology is onscreen eye-tracking. Today there are cameras that can accurately track the movements of your eyes as you scroll through, read, and view the contents of a web page on a computer, pad or phone. This technology can be used to communicate, to play games, and for other purposes, one of which is helping the computer to "learn about you" by tracking how many nanoseconds your gaze lingers on one part of the computer screen versus another. As if that isn't enough, we have Muse and iBrain, headband-like devices that allow a person to communicate through brainwaves alone. Both of these technologies—eye-tracking and brainwave monitoring—were developed to help profoundly physically disabled people, such as Dr. Stephen Hawking, function in both the real world and on computers. For instance, eye-tracking technology combined with an onscreen keyboard allows someone like Hawking to readily explore web pages, write, and otherwise communicate, while Muse and iBrain allow that same person to more effectively steer a wheelchair, turn on lights, or change the TV channel. Of course, the sexnological applications are practically end-

< 98 >

less. For instance, savvy pornographers will be able to use eye-tracking software as a way to figure out what most profoundly arouses you, automatically taking you to images and videos that mirror your deepest even subconscious desires. It won't even matter if you are consciously aware of your interest, because the computer will know and take you there. Furthermore, with a headband and a willing partner, those separated by distance will be able to merely think about stimulating their special someone and, using any number of teledildonic devices, those thoughts will become action.

The technology doesn't stop there, either. The KissPhone allows you to receive digital kisses, ostensibly from your wife, boyfriend, or grandmother. Basically, the person on one end of the digital connection kisses his or her phone, and that device measures lip pressure, temperature, movement, and so on, and then transmits that information so the KissPhone at the other end can re-create it. No, we are not kidding. It's hardly a leap to envision a digitally accessed bank of movie star and porn performer kisses—and more—available for a price, of course. And very soon people will be able to experience their entire partner, not just his or her lips, in a "tech-bed." Sheets and sleepwear are being designed with special fibers that produce sensory responses, allowing people to "feel" the sensations of their partner no matter how far away the other person might be. And should you become less aroused by the physical reality of your long-term partner's looks, no problem. Developers are hard at work creating contact lenses that can change the way a person appears to the viewer (unbeknownst to the person being observed).

Man + Machine

While researching her latest book, Sherry Turkle, director of the Initiative on Society and Self at the Massachusetts Institute of Technology (MIT), found more than a few people who were more interested in virtual and/or robotic girlfriends, boyfriends, and spouses than real-life versions of the same. "They felt that people had failed them, and that a robot would be a safer choice."[24] In truth, virtual girlfriends and boyfriends are already popular in Japan. One man even held a live commitment ceremony with his virtual girlfriend utilizing a dating simulation

< 99 >

game called Love Plus. "There are even resorts … where one can go on 'vacation' with these fantasy women [or men]," Turkle says.[25]

And, if you weren't aware, there are already robots designed and built to wash your hair, serve you tea, and mow your lawn. How much longer before Rosie—the walking, talking, emoting robot maid from the 1960s cartoon *The Jetsons*—is real? And what happens when Rosie's manufacturer decides she needs to look like a life-size Barbie doll, complete with pliable breasts and a vagina? And if Rosie the Robot who looks like Barbie and has a real-feel superskin vagina is personality-programmed to act as if she adores you, then what? Do robot girlfriends sound okay to you? What about robot wives that never express needs of their own?

Scientist David Levy, an internationally recognized expert on artificial intelligence and president of the International Computer Games Association, predicts that by 2050 technology will have progressed to the point where "humans will fall in love with robots, humans will marry robots, and humans will have sex with robots, all in [what will be regarded as] 'normal' extensions of our feelings of love and sexual desire for other humans."[26] And Levy is not alone in thinking humans can and will interact on a very real emotional level with technology. In her PBS documentary *Digital Nation: Life on the Virtual Frontier*, Rachel Dretzin states, "We've done studies with children where they see themselves swimming around with whales in a virtual reality. A week later, half of them will believe that they swam with whales."[27] Children also respond to "therapeutic contact" with a robot. Japanese researchers, for example, have shown that well-programmed robots can improve a child's mood and get antisocial children to interact more with other children and their caregivers.[28] And robots don't get annoyed, impatient, or disappointed when children are challenging, unresponsive, or just plain difficult, so what's not to love?

Marital Evolution?

Modern Western society no longer holds marriage in the high esteem it did just a few decades ago. A study by the Pew Research Center shows that 44 percent of Generation Y and 43 percent of Generation X actually

< 100 >

view marriage as "archaic."[29] The survey also found that in 2008 only 26 percent of men and women in their twenties were married, compared with 68 percent in 1960. Among all adults in 1960, 72 percent were married, compared to 52 percent in 2008. Clearly, marriage is no longer the be-all, end-all it was thought to be in the mid-twentieth century. Perhaps this should not be surprising, as the loving nuclear family model demonstrated in the 1950s and '60s on popular television shows like *Leave It to Beaver* and *Father Knows Best* has little to do with the reality of marriage throughout the ages.

Basically, for thousands of years marriage was primarily an economic (and occasionally political) contract negotiated and policed not by the two people involved, but by their families, communities, and churches. In "days of old" it took more than one person to make a household or family business thrive, so a mate's skills, resources, and participation were valued every bit as highly as (if not more highly than) that person's personality and physical appearance. The almost universal need for a household/business "partner" was that extreme. The post-WWII economic boom that allowed many U.S. families to survive on the income of a single breadwinner—almost always the husband, with the wife taking care of the home and children—is, historically speaking, an aberration.

As Stephanie Coontz writes in her enlightening book, *Marriage: A History*, "For most of history it was inconceivable that people would choose their mates on the basis of something as fragile and irrational as love and then focus all their sexual, intimate, and altruistic desires on the resulting marriage. In fact, many historians, sociologists, and anthropologists used to think romantic love was a recent Western invention."[30] In an interview published in the *Atlantic*, Coontz said, "We are without a doubt in the midst of an extraordinary sea change. The transformation is momentous—immensely liberating and immensely scary. When it comes to what people actually want and expect from marriage and relationships, and how they organize their sexual and romantic lives, all the old ways have broken down."[31]

In the simplest terms, monogamous relationships are now thought of by many younger people in terms of *what is lost* rather than what is

< 101 >

gained. Some young people view monogamy as a restriction on person-al freedoms, including the freedom to do what they want, when they want, on the Internet. The anonymity, affordability, and accessibility of sex and romance online has created a veritable amusement park of "adult" activity, and many men and women, especially digital natives, would rather live in this newfound sexual wonderland than settle down into a traditional long-term monogamous relationship.

This lack of interest in marriage is today most prominent among college-educated, digital native females. At the very least these women want to marry later in life than did past generations, perhaps to ensure financial independence for both parties once married, not just for the male partner. Many of these women are fully engaged in the burgeon-ing "digital hookup" culture as a way of getting their sexual/intimacy needs met. It some ways this trend is the logical outcome of the feminist movement's merger with modern technology. As Hanna Rosin, author of *The End of Men: And the Rise of Women*, writes in the *Atlantic*:

> Single young women in their sexual prime ... are for the first time in history more successful, on average, than the single young men around them. They are more likely to have a college degree and, in aggregate, they make more money. What makes this remarkable development possible is not just the pill or legal abortion but the whole new landscape of sexual freedom—the ability to delay marriage and have temporary relationships that don't derail education or career. To put it crudely, *feminist prog-ress right now largely depends on the existence of the hookup culture* [emphasis added]. And to a surprising degree, it is women—not men—who are perpetuating this culture, especially in school en-vironments, cannily manipulating their emotional and sexual needs to make success their first priority, always keeping their own ends in mind. For college girls in the 21st century, ending up with an overly serious suitor is nearly as painful and trou-blesome as was an accidental pregnancy in the 19th: a danger to be avoided at all costs, lest it get in the way of a promising future.[32]

< 102 >

This attitude is the exact opposite of what society taught women to want and expect from men/college/dating a mere generation ago, when young females were expected to be more focused on finding a man, getting "pinned," getting married, and having children than on developing a career. So here too we are seeing an evolving generation gap regarding sex, intimacy, relationships, dating, and romance.

The short- and long-term effects of this new tech-driven attitude toward relationships, intimacy, and marriage are at this point unknown. On the one hand, loving couples can now develop and maintain their relationships in ways that weren't possible just a few years ago. On the other hand, some people may choose to eschew real-world intimacy, opting instead for virtual sex, as it presents fewer emotional challenges and a greater sense of control. No matter how real the technology, people who are physically, socially, and mentally healthy seem, over time, to find the digital universe two-dimensional and unfulfilling, grow bored with it and long for the intimate emotional connections that can only be found in the real world. That said, as sexnology proliferates and improves, our expectations of real-world sexual partners will also evolve, and *real-world partners may not be able to keep pace*. After all, it is human nature to seek and/or create more refined sources of pleasure (refined cocaine, refined sugar, refined gaming and gambling via the Internet, and so on), and if the most pleasurable sexual and/or romantic experience involves a computer or robot rather than an actual human being, so be it.

So what is the future of dating, mating, sex, marriage, and parenting when computer-based interactions are simpler, more immediately available, and more pleasurable than being with a live person? Truthfully, only time will tell.

< 103 >

CHAPTER FIVE

Online Vulnerability: The Dark Side of the Force

Give a person a fish, and you feed him for a day.
Teach him to use the Internet, and he won't bother you for weeks.
—Revised Biblical adage, author unknown

The Internet and its related technologies have in fewer than three decades brought previously unimaginable changes in the way we live, work, entertain, and celebrate while simultaneously bringing cultural exposure to millions around the globe. Our evolving cultural reliance on digital technology is encouraging the beginnings of a near *one-world* community, allowing for the rapid dissemination of information in real time and the ability to build community, find support, and seek knowledge regardless of our location or the structure of our political systems. As a direct result, we have more opportunities for interconnectivity and cultural competence. Family, friends, and communities can remain connected and interwoven even if separated by continents. Business and professional communication worldwide is almost instantaneously and straightforwardly accomplished. Even the age-old process of meeting, dating, and mating has been meaningfully, if not permanently, altered for people of all ages and orientations.

The Not-So-Good Life: Online
Regrettably, where there is sunshine a little rain must also fall. Without becoming mired in pessimism or absolutes, we must acknowledge that despite our very human and understandable enthusiasm for *almost any* new technological advances, there are inevitably problems that come

< 105 >

along with them. For example, trains, planes, and automobiles have greatly facilitated human commerce and interconnectivity, but their existence has also resulted in accident-related deaths, time and energy lost to travel challenges, overdependence on foreign sources of energy, and the pollution of our air and water. Similarly, the digital world has its drawbacks. Some of the negative effects of becoming overly pulled into online life may include the following:

- invasion of privacy
- social isolation and loneliness
- potential disconnection among friends and family
- depersonalized business and professional relationships
- diminished physical activity
- information oversaturation
- inaccurate data being presented and perceived as fact
- potentially diminished social skill development
- child and adult safety risks
- risk for consumer abuse and fraud
- potential manipulation and abuse of online dating, mating, and relating
- online gambling, addictive or compulsive problems with online gaming, online porn, and access to casual sex
- distorted views of human sexuality and intimacy
- disrupted relationship intimacy
- relationship infidelity

Keep it Short and Sweet

So let's start this discussion with something small … our fingers. "In another few years, children will be born with tiny fingers except for their thumbs," an older man jokingly predicted while observing a group of teenagers texting each other, thumbs moving at lightning speed. He then recalled his own stumbling efforts to text his grandson, who had long ceased answering his cell phone or even responding to voicemail. In general, it seems digital natives prefer texting over talking, primarily because texting gives them more control over the interaction. In an

< 106 >

in-person or phone conversation, those engaged are "stuck" with an *interactive* exchange, meaning they have much less control over the content and length of the conversation. By comparison texting is a "no muss, no fuss" format, as it does not require an *interactive* response.

One meaningful concern about texts, along with emails, IMs, and tweets, is that this form of communication deprives the recipient of the kinds of visual and auditory cues that can only be perceived in person. One young woman explains it this way:

> I exchange dozens of texts daily but I feel like something is missing. When I get a text, I wonder, *What are they feeling? Are they upset?* If they're feeling angry, they may read anger in what I wrote, even if I didn't intend that. It's hard to read emotions in texts. If they just write "OK," and nothing more, are they annoyed? Are they neutral? If they don't add some emotional language or at least an emoticon to their message, I often don't know what they mean. The lack of emotional context when texting really bothers me. Yes, it does make communication faster, but it also seems to lack both nuance and quality.

Another man comments on his work-related email and texts:

> I can often feel overwhelmed by a never-ending barrage of daily digital communication, mostly email, but also text messages. And when I send email, I've noticed that I seem to be easily misperceived, like the person isn't quite reading the intended, underlying emotional framework of my messages. Sometimes it takes a few emails back and forth just to clarify those kinds of misperceptions. Today, I'm very careful when emailing or texting to not say anything negative or use language that could be misconstrued. There is something about the written word that seems to carry a lot more weight than something that is simply stated aloud.

< 107 >

Lonely + Isolated = More Narcissistic?

Anyone can experience loneliness, even when they're not physically alone. The truth is loneliness is less about physical isolation than about feeling emotionally disconnected. For example, many people report feeling lonely even when at a crowded party. One of the underlying evolutionary purposes of feeling lonely is that it motivates us to reach out and connect—to be the social and communal beings humans have always had to be in order to survive and thrive.

In modern society, loneliness can manifest both emotionally and physically. Research consistently demonstrates an inverse relationship between social isolation and health. Socially isolated people are:

- less likely to exercise
- more likely to be obese
- more likely to be depressed
- more likely to struggle with a combination of addiction and depression
- likely to die younger
- more likely to show early signs of dementia
- more likely to suffer from poor sleep[1]

Although it is easier than ever today to locate and connect with others, many people fail to do so, in part because our electronic means of communication (both sent and received) seem to encourage a greater focus on self than in the past. In other words, digital communication by its very nature encourages users to engage in a more frequent and greater display of narcissistic or self-focused engagement.

In truth, many Facebook users use social media essentially as a public scrapbook, posting endless photographs and descriptions of their moment-to-moment life activities. People can spend hours, even days of "social time" all by themselves, organizing images, updating profiles, and otherwise documenting and reshaping their lives for others to view and comment on. In other words, these posts do not present a direct invitation to interact. They are self-statements and, as such, are inherently narcissistic by any standard.

< 108 >

However, it is also worth noting that within any evolving new form of communication there are likely some unwritten rules that are not readily revealed simply by reading the content. For example, if I write about myself and my world in a social media platform hoping that others who share my interests and beliefs will reach out to form a new community with me, then those actions clearly are less inherently narcissistic and more about working within the structure of that new medium toward connection. As is always the case, *wherever we go, there we are*. In other words, self-focused people will likely bring their self-focus online, whereas those wishing to reach out to others will likely find the connections they seek.

Nevertheless, despite our ever-increasing digital interconnectivity, current research reveals that more of us express feeling more detached and alone than ever before, and finding that our current social connections leave us feeling increasingly more empty.[2] This phenomenon affects digital immigrants most of all. To this point, a recent AARP study showed that 35 percent of adults over age forty-five reported feeling *chronically lonely* in 2010, compared with 20 percent of the same population a mere decade earlier.[3] Currently, about one-fifth of all Americans report feeling "unhappy with their lives" due to loneliness.[4] This is happening against a backdrop of unprecedented interconnectivity, in which millions of people are emailing, texting, instant messaging, tweeting, and posting dozens of times daily.

Research in Australia (where nearly half the population is on Facebook) reveals that people who are identified as being more neurotic and isolated tend to spend more time on Facebook.[5] Do they log onto Facebook more often because they feel lonely and/or isolated? Are they neurotic and isolated because they spend more time on Facebook than interacting in person with family and friends? Or do they, perhaps, rely on Facebook to escape unhappy family and/or social situations? Unfortunately, the study does not provide a definitive answer. Nevertheless, it seems logical to conclude that for some people live connections and relationships are being compromised because of time spent online.

Many people report feeling "obsessed" with Facebook and/or other social media. Recent research indicates that nearly half of all digital na-

< 109 >

tive Facebook users check their account within minutes of waking up.[6] Some users "collect" followers, celebrating each additional friend and follower. Sadly, the self-worth of those whose lives are deeply entwined in social media can often be directly tied to their "numbers" on Facebook and/or Twitter. In therapy, such people often report that their emotional stability and self-esteem waxes and wanes in direct relation to how these virtual communities respond to each of their carefully phrased posts and tweets. Being "unfriended" by a meaningful Facebook friend or Twitter follower can leave a vulnerable person in full remorse mode wondering, *What did I do wrong?* This occurs even though that friend is someone that they never directly communicated with or met in person. People already suffering from anxiety or depression can find their conditions exacerbated because of this online popularity contest.

The Australian study also confirmed the general belief that Facebook users tend to demonstrate more narcissistic and exhibitionistic personality traits than non-users, displaying self-absorption, attention seeking, grandiosity, and a lack of empathy.[7] Writing in great detail about their lives and activities, many Facebook users expect others to immediately read, appreciate, and respond to their posts. Unfortunately, those exhibitionistic tendencies can at times lead to overly elaborate, inappropriate, and sometimes even dangerous online activity. These men and women don't seem to realize that online narcissistic oversharing can be a serious turnoff.

One potential disadvantage to those more focused on virtual connections than on live interaction is that real-world experiences with other people (both positive and negative) presents genuine opportunities for learning. In person, someone is likely to correct you, interrupt your monologue, or simply distance himself or herself from you—any and all of which can be painful and upsetting but also likely to lead to insight and personal growth. A major problem with living online is that when others get tired of your behavior they are likely to just "un-friend" or "un-follow" you, often without your learning why and thereby growing from the experience. In other words, online interactivity at present appears to offer fewer opportunities for personal growth than in-person experiences.

< 110 >

Smartphones = The New TV

Of great concern to parents and educators who were raising children in the now distant 1950s and 1960s was that television might spell the end of family communication. In retrospect, it turns out that when families viewed TV programs *together* the content gave them an opportunity to have a shared experience to comment about, and learn from. In other words, it actually provided an opportunity to engage. The feared and expected demise of the American family related to the boob tube simply never came to pass.

Similarly, parents today worry about the effect on their kids, of online sexual content, violent video and war games, social media, and hours and hours of texting. And unlike television, mobile devices demand the user's exclusive attention, even if just temporarily. And these devices are increasingly finding their way into every aspect of people's lives. Polls taken in 2012 showed that 50 percent of Americans owned smartphones, and 58 percent of that group reported checking these devices at least hourly, often at what one might consider "inappropriate" times. For example, 30 percent reported using their phones while sharing a meal, 39 percent while using the bathroom, and 9 percent during a religious service. If they were forced to choose, 21 percent said they would rather give up sex than surrender their phones![8]

Note this all-too-common scenario:

Ralph and his new wife, Rita, flew across the United States to celebrate the fortieth birthday of their son-in-law, Bill, with Bill's wife Judy, and their children. For this special event, Judy prepared a lavish, formal dinner for her in-laws, served on her finest china. Bill and Judy's children drew a huge "Happy Birthday, Dad!" sign, which they hung above the dinner table. As they ate, Ralph, Rita, Judy, and the children engaged in animated conversation, catching up on events of the past year. Bill, however, despite being the de facto star of the party, with loved ones all around, sat in relative silence throughout the meal. He did eat and offer the occasional nod, acknowledging the conversation going on around him, but for the most part he spent

< 111 >

the meal focused on his smartphone, reading and responding to overseas work-related texts and emails. By dinner's end, Rita had gotten to know her new daughter-in-law and grandkids better, but she had learned nothing about her new stepson Bill, nor had he learned anything about her. The following evening, as the four adults dined at an upscale restaurant, it was more of the same: Ralph, Rita, and Judy conversed throughout the meal while Bill mostly read and responded to incoming emails and texts. On both occasions, it appeared to Rita that only she and Ralph seemed to notice that Bill's thoughts were elsewhere— that he was physically there yet not fully present. What struck Rita as curious was that no one said a word about her stepson's emotional absence and seeming distance from his family. His activity appeared to be such an established part of the family's dinner/life routine that it was simply the norm.

This sort of *intermittent disconnection*—attending to technology while simultaneously in a social setting—appears to be increasingly tolerated as part of personal, business, and professional interactions. In fact, for digital natives it is most likely to become the norm. Nevertheless, this dual social and digital focus does not come without consequences, such as:

- Rita headed back to the East Coast with negative feelings about her new stepson Bill, feeling that he didn't care enough to look up from his phone and really connect.
- Bill's children didn't get to experience their dad interacting with his own father (their grandfather), nor did they get to witness their dad's playful side at a special family event.
- Judy put a great deal of effort into the planning and execution of Bill's fortieth birthday, but Bill didn't seem to notice, leaving her feeling undervalued.

Bill, at the other end of the spectrum, felt proud of himself for having stayed (in his mind) in close touch with visiting family, the kids, and

< 112 >

Judy while also managing to keep up with work. This line of thinking was validated by his peers when he returned to work on Monday morning and they expressed appreciation for how "on top of things" he was, even when not physically in the office.

Today, in the midst of our techno-generational divide, this type of tech-disconnect is the stuff of strained familial bonds, friendships, and disengaged parenting. But how will this scenario affect us in 2020, 2040 or even 2060? Will people grow up in a world where texting at dinner is as acceptable as salting one's French fries and will there be collateral damage to the future family unit? Who can tell? We don't know yet.

Online interaction or lack thereof does have the potential to cause other types of pain as well. As a recent *New York Times* article states, "When families fall apart in the Facebook age, social media can only add to the pain."[9] It's hard enough to be estranged from your children when there is no direct news from them, but it can be even harder when you learn through Facebook that your estranged child has gone through a significant life event without informing you. The effect of such impersonal communication only more acutely reminds those removed from the family tree how much they have become outsiders. "Out of touch, but never out of sight on the Internet," summarizes the article.[10] Constant online reminders like these can prevent emotional wounds from healing. Sure, you can choose not to look up your child or ex-stepdad on social media, but "staying away" can be incredibly difficult. Some loved ones simply can't help but check up on those they have loved deeply, looking for clues as to why they've been cut off and/or how they might re-engage.

Failed romantic relationships are much the same, as a recent *Huffington Post* blog bemoans:

> Social media is a continual highlight reel of your life with someone else, and sometimes that makes it hurt more. ... First there are the emails. The daily back and forth over new restaurants, decisions about a potential vacation. ... Or the chats—funny, random, stupid videos that now mean something beyond their comedic value. Thousands upon thousands. So what do you

< 113 >

do? Save them? Put them in the drawer with the photos? Comb through and delete, then permanently delete? Then you have the demon of Facebook. Unhooking your names if they were linked together to be splayed across the feed of everyone you ever knew. ... You're forced to look at evidence of you, because you recorded it everywhere. ... Instagram and Twitter can be even more trying.[11]

The point is, it's much more difficult now to erase a former loved one from your life than it was in the old days when you simply could stow the photo albums and gifts in a drawer or discard them and move on.

And the Doctor Is ... Where Exactly?

Another increasingly common example of disconnection now regularly takes place in an environment where nearly all of us already feel vulnerable—our own doctor's office. Sadly, lack of eye contact with one's physician while in his or her presence is an increasingly common experience. Directly related to the constraints of medical insurance carriers and the "business of healthcare," physicians more often choose or are required to maintain electronic medical records (EMRs) rather than writing down their notes in a paper chart. EMRs are easier to read (as it is true that most doctors' writing is illegible), can be transmitted electronically, can be more easily analyzed, and are easier to store and share than the paper charts of old. Unfortunately, the execution of EMRs is more than a little bit demanding. As a result, the doctor-patient relationship, which in the past always included careful and direct patient observation, is fast being replaced by a system where the doctor sits at his or her desk intellectually engaged yet emotionally disconnected from the patient, typing on a pad or device throughout their brief interaction.

One physician documented his experience with EMRs in a 2012 editorial in the *Journal of the American Medical Association*:

We must pick and click according to the EMR's pathways, rather than by following the patterns of learning, interaction and practice. All this searching and selecting takes time, a lot of

< 114 >

time. Not surprisingly, we (the doctors) find ourselves entering more and more data while we are trying to listen to and talk with our patients. You survive in this new system by giving the computer complete attention, the kind of attention we used to reserve for a patient. By default, the patient moves down to second place. As sad and horrifying as this sounds and feels, it is becoming the new reality. I went into medicine to work with people, but now I'm in front of a computer screen all day, managing systems. I still love my patients, but I hate how I'm spending my time.[12]

The 24/7 Work Environment

Advances in communication technology combined with the pressure to succeed in our highly competitive work environments poses numerous emotional and physical health risks to both children and adults. For instance, many businesses now either expect or even require their white-collar or management-level workers to be available online 24/7. In the digital age, there is no downtime from work. Bill's story of staying connected with work during his birthday celebration is a good example of this. This kind of 24/7 connectivity has the potential to fragment our ability to concentrate, increasing stress while ultimately decreasing productivity. Workers, especially digital immigrants, are fully turned on and tuned in, but their emotional and physical health may take a parallel tumble. Whether digital natives, those who've grown up with multitasking at the center of their existence, will respond to such situations with more defined boundaries or simply accept having to be at work 24/7 is yet unknown.

The Perpetual Texter

Not paying attention to the outside world because we are overly focused on technology is also of concern, especially among young people for whom multitasking is the norm. A 2011 Centers for Disease Control (CDC) survey found that 58 percent of high school seniors admitted to texting while driving, even thought it is now illegal in most states. The owner of a popular Arizona traffic school recently reported that

< 115 >

every student in his classes admitted to having close calls while texting and driving. These close calls included unknowingly crossing into an oncoming lane on a two-way street, nearly running off the road, and hitting parked cars. These problems increasingly sound like a lot worse than a "close call."[13] And kids aren't the only culprits who are texting and driving. Adults are doing it too.

Fact

For an adept texter, the average text message takes about five seconds to type. At fifty-five miles per hour, an automobile will travel the length of a football field before that texting driver hits the send key.

In the United States, texting has now eclipsed drunk driving as the primary cause of preventable auto fatalities. In response, most states have passed laws against texting or talking on a (non-Bluetooth) phone while driving, but these laws are very hard to enforce. Awareness of the issue is, however, rising. In Austin, TX, large digital freeway signs constantly project the following message: "You drive. You text. You die." Throughout the 2012 Summer Olympics, television networks aired numerous public service ads about the dangers of texting while driving. This challenge is pushing the auto and communications industries toward new solutions that will allow people to "more safely" drive while actively sending email and texts—which simply means that the actual phone won't be in your hand while you drive and work or socialize.

The Perpetual Sitter

A life lived online also affects physical health. All that sitting and standing around while texting, emailing, e-shopping, and telecommuting is more likely to keep you immobile than out running errands, meeting friends, or going to the "Y" for a swim. The often obsessive nature of online activity tends to keep us planted in our chairs as opposed to getting the activity—walking, jogging, yoga, or bicycling, for example—needed for optimum health. Take a moment to reflect on how many times you gave up an opportunity to be physically active because you were too

< 116 >

busy fulfilling that 24/7 job commitment or were unable/unwilling to leave your tablet, phone, or screen because your online activity was so much more appealing than the idea of actually moving around?

It is a fact that human technological development has negatively affected our physical health. This was true long before the Internet became an integral part of our lives. For example, obesity is a health epidemic in many modern countries. One major contributing factor to obesity is all those convenient elevators, escalators, and automobiles. These technologies evolved for our convenience and comfort, allow us to traverse ground with far less physical movement than in days of yore. Technology also affects the type of foods we eat and the way we eat them. For the most part, the foods we eat today have more refined grains, more salt, and more sugar than the "homemade" dishes of the past. They are less healthy (but take less time to prepare) than in the past, thus allowing us to "waste less productive time" as we can simply "grab" something to eat.

Adult Safety Online

Chapter 3 discussed potential risks to children in the digital universe and how parents can help. However, in many of the same ways as do our children, we adults (digital natives and immigrants alike) also face risks, such as lack of privacy, cyberstalking, deliberate misuse of intimate messages and sexts, dating scams, and financial scams.

Lack of Privacy

Many successful, intelligent, thoughtful, clear-headed people who would never consider giving out their social security number, credit information, or even birth date to an online stranger will, seemingly without a second thought, sext and text out their most intimate desires on their smartphone, often accompanied by high-definition photos of exposed genitalia (with faces attached), to a potential mate or sexual partner. Perhaps the fact that smartphones and other mobile devices don't look or act like traditional computers, as they lack a visible browser history, instills in users a false sense that they are invisible and cannot be traced. Or perhaps people naively think that Internet porn and hook-

< 117 >

up businesses are somehow ethically motivated to protect your privacy.

And why not think that? After all, most of the time when you join a website or download a phone app you receive a *click-it guarantee* that the personal information you provide will be securely maintained. But all that guarantee really means is that the service provider won't willingly hand off or sell your private login information, texts, or nude pics to other interested parties. It doesn't mean a hacker can't or won't access your information or that the provider won't go out of business, leaving all that data for another party to access (with no legal binding agreements). Plus, when you send a text of any kind, that data is not magically deleted immediately after being sent. Instead, it is stored in a faraway server for an indeterminate amount of time. How much time? Let's just say it's a lot longer than you might like. And as long as your most intimate sexual and romantic data are stored on that faraway server, you remain vulnerable. Very vulnerable.

Actually, the hacking of sex/dating websites and smartphone apps happens with almost frightening regularity. For example, in January 2012, Grindr was compromised by an Australian hacker who placed male users' personal chats, explicit photos, and other private information online. Days later, a seventeen-year-old hacker infiltrated a website operated by porn mega-provider Brazzers. The emails, usernames, and potentially embarrassing personal information of more than 350,000 Brazzers users may have been exposed. And soon after the Brazzers hack, YouPorn, one of the Internet's most popular porn sites, scrambled to deflect blame for the release of private login information to more than one million accounts. YouPorn insisted that its site was not hacked, blaming the information dump on a third-party chat provider. Either way, the damage was done. More than a million email addresses, passwords, and intimate preferences became public. In case you lost count, that's three major hacks of three different service providers within a very short period of time.

Most digital privacy invasions are performed by loved ones rather than hackers. One survey found that 76 percent of women and 69 percent of men would look at their partner's email if it were left open. And most of the time, your information doesn't even have to be "left open."[14]

< 118 >

Think about those seemingly innocuous questions you answer when you set up an online account. You answer those questions so that, in the event you forget your password, you can contact the service provider, answer a question, and retrieve the password. In other words, if you (or anyone else) can supply your mother's maiden name, the name of your first pet, and the name of your high school, then you *or anyone else* are in.

Cyberstalking

Cyberstalking is the deliberate abuse of the Internet or other electronic media to stalk or harass someone. Although a cyberstalker does not necessarily pose a physical threat (unless his or her activities escalate to real-world stalking), online stalkers can still cause a whole lot of psychological and emotional damage. They gather information about their potential victim and then use it to make various threats in electronic venues. Cyberstalkers, much like terrorists, generally want to control the victim, leaving that person feeling fearful and threatened. Perpetrators of domestic violence sometimes use cyberstalking as a way to continue controlling and terrorizing their victims after the spouse or partner has already left the relationship. Here are a few examples:

- A fired employee sent hundreds of emails containing (fake) pornographic images of the firm's vice president to the entire company. These were images the fired employee created with Photoshop but presented as genuine.
- A former boyfriend, angered at a woman's rejection, put fake ads that included her photo online, soliciting sex partners and giving her name, address, and phone number. As a result, she received hundreds of emails and phone calls from men hoping to have sex with her.
- A pedophile who assumed a teenage alias on a teen website became infatuated with a thirteen-year-old girl who had briefly responded to him. He fantasized that they had a serious relationship. He sent her dozens of daily messages for months, even though she did not answer.

< 119 >

Working to Halt Online Abuse (WHOA), www.haltabuse.org, collects demographic information on cyberstalking victims and perpetrators. In 2012, among the 394 victims identified, 80 percent were female and 69 percent were single. Of the harassers, 49 percent were male, 31 percent female, and 20 percent unknown. In 24 percent of the cases, the cyberstalker was an "ex," while 19 percent were online-only acquaintances. The two most common venues for the onset of harassment were email, in 31 percent of cases, and Facebook, in 16 percent of cases. Cyberstalking escalated in 83 percent of cases, becoming more virulent and eventually using multiple online venues.[15]

Cyberstalkers pursue their victims via:

- **Direct communication through email**—This is the most common kind of cyberstalking. It targets one individual and invades his or her private space.
- **Global communication through the Internet**—This activity includes public involvement. It may include impersonating the victim to incite others to contact him or her inappropriately.
- **Unauthorized control of another person's computer**—This involves obtaining access to everything on the victim's computer, logging every keystroke the victim makes, and the ability to view the victim's computer desktop screen in real time.
- **Personal threats**—This is an attempt to "expose" the victim via online posting of potentially embarrassing images or language.

Most states now have laws criminalizing cyberstalking. Also, the number of websites aimed at preventing cyberstalking and helping its victims is increasing. However, these laws vary greatly from state to state and country to country. In some places, inciting others to contact or harass a victim (as opposed to direct stalker contact) does not qualify as a crime. Clearly, the legal framework for cyberstalking is still evolving. The issue serves as a reminder that many problem behaviors that are

< 120 >

clearly illegal in the "real world" often lack consistent legal guidelines in the virtual world.

Adults and Sexting

Inarguably the most infamous case of adult sexting gone bad is that of former U.S. congressman Anthony Weiner, who resigned under pressure in 2011 after being publicly outed as having posted (on Twitter) nude self-photos taken in the congressional gym. And while that incident was accompanied by a national chorus of "What was he thinking?" (the answer being, "He wasn't,") former Congressman Weiner is hardly alone in this activity. *A recent survey found that more than one-quarter of the adults who own smartphones have sent or received a sext.* The largest percentage of those found to be sexting, 40 percent, was among men ages eighteen to thirty-four (male digital natives). Even among older people (fifty-five years and older), 10 percent reported having sexted.[16]

Considering that 69 percent of all smartphone owners report losing their phone at some point, and that everything sent via one's phone "lives on," a whole lot of people today are risking discovery of highly intimate online communication. And it should serve as no surprise that the discovery of such material can and often does produce profound, adverse consequences. Just ask the former congressman and failed New York City mayoral candidate.

Financial Scammers: Part One

The ability to communicate via digital technology is especially valuable during disasters, when people are desperate to find family members, when there is a need for aid to disaster victims, and when it's crucial to quickly disseminate life-saving information. Tragedies bring out the best in most of us and, unfortunately, the worst in a rare few. For example, on December 14, 2012, twenty-six people, including twenty children, were killed in a school shooting in Newtown, CT. Within twenty-four hours at least two fake "victim support websites" were put up, purportedly to collect money for the families of victims. In reality, the purpose was to swindle donations from generous souls. Similar financial scams were perpetrated following recent major hurricanes. Of course, hustlers have

< 121 >

been around forever. The only difference today is that they no longer need to knock on your door for a stolen donation; they can simply drop you an email.

Couples seeking to adopt children provide another golden opportunity for online scams. Although the Internet can be an amazingly helpful tool for arranging child adoptions, it can also defraud vulnerable, gullible people. For example, one deceptive "adoption agency" cheated couples out of hundreds of thousands of dollars by promising to arrange adoptions in Kazakhstan. Once the deposit money was sent, the "agency" claimed that numerous obstacles prevented the adoptions from taking place, but alas the down payment was gone forever.[17]

Not a day goes by without at least one of us receiving an email supposedly sent by a high-ranking government official from a distant country explaining that he or she has come into possession of a very large sum of money. The sender offers to give us 10 percent or even 50 percent of this fortune if only we supply them with access to our bank account (so they can transfer their funds into it) or send them a relatively small sum, say $1,000, which is what it will cost to "get their money out of the country." Most of us sigh or laugh at this well-known scam and delete the email; however, an unfortunate few are bilked. And then there are the emails from "friends" whose names we recognize (because their email accounts were hacked and we were on their email list), making desperate pleas for money to be sent to them abroad as they have been "robbed" or are in some trouble.

Over time, Internet scammers have become more and more adept at targeting specific populations. The elderly, who are often less computer savvy and more in need of money, are the demographic group most likely to be reeled in when dollars are the bait. The unsuspecting person is somehow convinced to send the scammer money, and then send more, each request supposedly being the final one. Eventually, some find that their bank accounts have been emptied out. Far too many senior citizens have lost their life savings, and even their homes in this sad form of fraud and theft.

< 122 >

Manipulation and Abuse of the Online Dating Experience

Some unscrupulous individuals use romance as bait. Consider Linda's story:

Two years past a painful divorce, Linda, a fifty-five-year old university professor who loves travel, joined an online dating site. She soon was matched with Andries, a charming, sophisticated Dutch man living in Amsterdam. He told Linda that he was a retired businessman who had traveled extensively and now had lots of free time. The couple emailed daily and had lengthy phone conversations several times a week. At the start of this exchange, Linda felt energized, youthful, and optimistic about the way her life was going. After three months, Andries announced that he was planning a trip to the United States and was hoping to meet Linda in person.

As the time of their meeting grew closer, their emails became more personal. Andries, now in essence an "online boyfriend," eventually asked Linda for a few intimate photos. Convinced by now that they were clearly a couple, she emailed him a nude photo taken from the waist up. The following day, he demanded she send him a large amount of money or he would email her photo to every member of her university department. Shocked and scared by these blackmail threats and realizing what a mistake she had made, Linda contacted the International Criminal Police Organization, turning over to them her entire history of online communication with Andries. As a likely result of her brave action, Linda never heard from Andries again, nor was her intimate photo disseminated.

Linda's story proves that being well educated does not prevent someone from being harmed online. Would doing a background check on someone like Andries early on have informed Linda who she was really dealing with? Maybe. It is quite simple to perform an online search to check out a potential dating partner, and it's even possible to do a

< 123 >

more extensive background check. If you are in the virtual dating world you may well consider going the extra mile and doing such research when any new long-distance romance begins to seriously flower.

Linda's story also highlights an important feature of online romance. Inherent to Internet communication is the concept of *fantasy*. With only words, images, and perhaps a short video as fodder for a considered response, it is easy for a healthy person, one eager to find a mate, to indulge in *extensive fantasizing* about another person. Yet those fantasies may or may not survive a live meeting. When online, people consistently and intentionally shade the truth (lie) about various aspects of themselves. Age, weight, and personal characteristics are a breeze to manipulate in the virtual world.

Furthermore, the very nature of how we email, text, and otherwise interact in the digital universe produces a skewed version of who we really are. For instance, by its very nature, chatting by email or IM forces you to take turns. If the other person is someone who constantly interrupts and dominates a live discussion, you wouldn't know that from a virtual experience. Internet communication is sequential, so the opportunity to interrupt is eliminated, resulting in everyone appearing polite. Moreover, because email, texting, and IMs allow each person to formulate thoughts and express them optimally, this form of communication can as readily disguise social awkwardness, shyness, and plain old poor social skills. Just as telephone conversations lack important visual cues, such as a person's facial expressions and body language in response to what you say, the Internet does too. Skype and webcams can and do provide additional cues, but they still allow users to end an uncomfortable exchange with no more than a swift click.

Financial Scammers: Part Two

In the digital universe it is all too easy, especially if you are in a vulnerable emotional state, to "fall in love" with someone you barely know. This tendency has produced the latest way for unscrupulous people to take advantage of others—Internet romance scams preying on a potential victim's emotional attachment and his or her desire to help a "loved one" in need. The victims of these crimes experience two significant

< 124 >

losses. First, physical losses in the form of money or some other gift given. Second, emotional losses, in the form of feeling stupid, betrayed, violated and yet still alone.

Typically romance scammers initiate relationships through online dating sites. Then, after months of virtual communication to establish an emotional bond, they persuade their victims to send gifts or money (usually by saying they need money for an emergency medical procedure or to buy a plane ticket they'll use to visit the victim). Sadly, these scams are often effective. A recent British study found that as of mid-2011 approximately 230,000 British citizens had reported falling victim to this crime.[18] Because of the victim's feelings of embarrassment, it is highly likely that these offenses are vastly underreported.

Most romance scam perpetrators operate out of foreign countries; at present Ghana appears to be the epicenter of such scamming. One woman who spoke publicly about her case is Jody Buell, a fifty-three-year-old who in 2008 was matched on a dating site, eHarmony.com, with a supposedly very compatible man. Their relationship blossomed via email, IMs, and phone conversations. After three months of "dating," the man told her he was traveling to Ghana to open an office. In Ghana, he purportedly developed both financial and health problems requiring emergency funds. Buell sent him over $10,000 before coming to realize the entire interaction had been a scam.[19]

Romance Scams Quiz

If you've been on a dating or social networking site recently, take this quick four-question quiz to see whether you might be dealing with a romance scammer.

1. Has someone "fallen in love" with you even though you've never met in person?
2. Do they claim to be from the United States but working overseas?
3. Have they asked you for money or to cash a check?
4. Were they coming to visit you soon but an event prevented them from doing so?

If you answered "yes" to any of the questions, proceed with caution.

< 125 >

Buell used her experience to help others form Romancescams.org offering "support, education, and healing for all who find their way here." Although the Internet helped create her problem in the first place, the same outlet also made it possible for her to quickly reach out to other people around the world who needed to better protect themselves.

Disturbed Relationship Intimacy

Caitlin Dewey, a student who won first prize in a 2011 *New York Times* writing contest about what love is like for digital natives, described her online romantic experience in an essay entitled "Even in Real Life, There Were Screens Between Us."[20] At a web journalism conference, Caitlin had briefly met Will, another student who lived three states away, and upon returning home they got to know each other almost entirely on Skype, video chatting nightly. Caitlin wrote:

> In the safety of my apartment, I could see Will but I couldn't touch him. I could summon him when I wanted to talk, but I never knew him in any light other than the one from his bedside lamp. This phenomenon worked in my favor as well. I could call him after a few drinks, when I felt sufficiently talkative and social; I could avoid him if I had videos to edit or blog posts to write. I could say whatever I wanted and risk awkwardness, because at the end of the conversation, one click of the mouse would shut him out of my room. The irony is that we flock to the Internet for this type of safe, sanitized intimacy, but we want something entirely different. No matter how much you love someone's blog or Twitter feed, it isn't their posts you actually want.

It seems likely that what most people "actually want" is to be together IRL. Caitlin certainly did. It took some time but eventually she rented a car and drove 540 miles to spend a weekend with Will.

> He stood waiting at the side of the street while I parked my car. We kissed on the cold blustery sidewalk. Mostly I felt relieved.

< 126 >

I thought, "This works in real life. This means something." But after we kissed and ate pizza and went back to his house, we struggled for things to talk about. In real life, Will stared off at nothing while I talked. In real life, he had no questions about the drive or my work or the stuff that waited for me when I went back to school. He took me out for dinner and read his e-mail while we waited for our food. He apologized profusely, but still checked his Web site's traffic stats while we sat in his living room. He took me to a party at his friend's house where they proceeded to argue for hours about Web design while I sat on a futon and stared at the ceiling, drunk and bored and terribly concerned that I looked thinner online than in life.

That weekend marked the end of Caitlin and Will's relationship. After that, she never wanted to see him again. Why not? What was missing? What do people really want in a relationship? Perhaps the answer is intimacy. Jennifer Schneider, one of the authors of this book, has previously defined the somewhat nebulous concept of intimacy as follows:

> Intimacy evolves out of our willingness to let a partner really know us, to exchange unfiltered honest feelings and thoughts, while tolerating our very human fear of being judged, criticized, and abandoned. Intimacy requires vulnerability, and trust can only arise out of vulnerable, open, and consistent mutual experiences that occur over time.[21]

Conducting a long-distance relationship has now been possible for several centuries via letter writing, the telegraph, and the telephone. But little has been written about long-term committed relationships that have evolved or been conducted solely through online or social media interactions. It seems logical, and even likely, at least to those born before 1980, that spending time in the physical presence of that other person, "being together" at least intermittently, is a requirement for creating and maintaining long-term intimate relationships. As far as we know today, evolving a cherished relationship entirely without face-to-

< 127 >

face, in person contact appears to be extremely difficult. The questions we face now are:

- Can webcams and other rapidly advancing virtual devices provide the personal contact required for meaningful, long-term romance?
- Will our tech-driven, increasingly lifelike virtual experiences reduce or even eliminate a barrier (space and time) that was a past requirement for long-term love and romance?

Infidelity and the Internet

Research universally suggests that somewhere between 10 and 20 percent of both men and women in committed long-term relationships and marriages are sexually and/or romantically unfaithful to their spouse or partner. Of course, today the concept of "cheating" has become a bit more malleable than back in the days when infidelity actually meant having *physical contact*. Frequent cybersex users share the following:

- I spend time in online romantic chats that turn sexual a lot more than I have sex with my husband these days. The more time I spend online, the less interested I am in him as a sexual or romantic partner.
- I have withdrawn from my primary relationship. I can't wait for my wife to fall asleep so I can go online.
- I tend to push away my spouse's fears about the porn I view. Lately I have stopped telling her about it altogether as she tends to hound me to stop when I do.

So what exactly does it mean to be unfaithful in today's digital world? Is live physical interaction still required, or does a webcam encounter with someone half a world away count just as much? What about pornography, webcam flirting or using Facebook and/or smartphone apps like Skout, Blendr, and Ashley Madison? Let's face it, for digital immigrants (and even some digital natives) it's a new and confusing world. What defines infidelity remains, to the authors of this

< 128 >

book, as clear today as it was when Monica Lewinsky first stored away her stained little blue dress. Infidelity can be simply defined as *the breaking of trust caused by the keeping of secrets in an intimate relationship*. For example, it is not a sexual dalliance itself that causes the most disruption to an intimate relationship, but rather the lying that it takes to carry that out.

Cheating, of course, is nothing new. In all likelihood, people have sought out sexual hookups outside of their primary relationships since the beginning of time. However, the Internet, social media, and the related recent proliferation of "adult friend-finder" (sexual hookup) smartphone apps, some of which were specifically designed to facilitate infidelity, have rapidly, drastically, and permanently altered the cheating landscape. For one thing, evidence of infidelity is now easier to set-up, hide and deny for a multitude of reasons.

Sadly, many men and women don't realize or want to see how their online sexual behavior effects the long-term emotional life of a trusting spouse. There seems to be a significant disconnect between how "digital" cheaters perceive the effects of his or her behavior and the actual experience of his or her mate. Consider the words of Angela, a thirty-eight-year-old woman married for fifteen years to Jack, a man who views and masturbates to pornography on a daily basis:

> My husband does not believe he has a problem. He feels it's no big deal since he claims he's being faithful to me. Jack thinks all he needs is a more accepting wife. I'm not sure that he really wants a wife at all—at least in the traditional sense. I think a maid would do it for him. Most of the time I feel more replaced by that machine and all the images it endlessly churns out than if he were having a real affair. At least then I'd know what I'm up against. But how can I compete with this ever-changing visual tide of young, nubile women—all available to him whenever he presses "power-on"?

Angela clearly disagrees with Jack's definition of "faithful." And this is the exact dilemma that many long-term couples now face, es-

< 129 >

pecially couples who are digital immigrants. With the increasing availability of electronic intimacy and virtual sexuality, what exactly does it mean to be faithful and/or unfaithful? Because of this confusion, spouses and partners can feel both anger and fear, along with a sense that the virtual sex has inflicted as much pain to them as a live affair, if not more. Yet in this "new" world, spouses—both male and female—also question themselves, wondering whether their feelings are normal responses to feeling cheated on or simply a sign of their own jealous pathology. Angela continues:

> How can I know right from wrong here? Am I right to feel abandoned and cheated on? Or is Jack's online sexual behavior truly inconsequential to us as a couple, which is what he keeps telling me at every turn?

Online sexual activities (when kept secret or carried out despite a spouse's wishes for it to stop) can cause a great deal of distress to long-term partners, even if the user fails to see the behavior as problematic. Frequent cybersex users often: (1) withdraw emotionally and physically from their real-life relationships, and (2) keep secrets and lie repeatedly, denying their partner's perceptions, and minimizing their emotional pain. Withdrawal and denial are the key elements of an affair, no matter if it takes place online or in the flesh. Betrayed partners routinely report experiencing the same negative emotional consequences whether it's "virtual cheating" or a real-life affair.

Blaming the Medium

For many people who have experienced the downside of digital technology, there is a tendency to blame the technology, much as those who supported prohibition laws in the 1920s blamed the alcohol itself rather than the drinker. However, blaming the computer is somewhat shortsighted. Certainly, without Twitter and a smartphone, congressman Anthony Weiner would not have been able to post images of his genitals hoping to attract available women. But pre-Internet, it seems likely that someone who was going to act out in this way would have done some-

< 130 >

thing else that was just as damaging, like flirting with co-workers or hiring escorts. Do we blame the car for the car accident?

Internet and digital technology in and of itself cannot be blamed for causing the problems described in this chapter, nor should modern technology be condemned *as the reason* humans act the ways they do. Just as it is not the fault of the whiskey if the drinker becomes a drunk, our online problems remain mirrored refractions back to us of the people we are. This includes both the good and the bad no matter the medium of their expression.

After all, a machine (at least to this point), remains a machine, something in perpetual need of a human being to direct its action. The machines of today can both escalate our problems in light speed while simultaneously illuminating them for all to see. But it remains the intent, beliefs and actions of the operator which bear full responsibility for any ensuing pain, potential harm, drama or joy caused—and not the machine itself.

< 131 >

CHAPTER SIX

Technology and the "New" Addictions

Why is it drug addicts and computer aficionados are both called users?
—*Clifford Stoll, scientist and author*

When people hear the word *addiction*, they typically think of someone dependent on substances like nicotine, alcohol, prescription medications, crystal meth, cocaine, or heroin. And addiction is the right term. If you consistently ingest certain substances that produce feelings of pleasure or intense emotions or make you feel numb, your body will begin to crave this substance and you can become both psychologically and physically hooked. Such substances are incredibly difficult to quit once a person becomes addicted. Prolonged abuse can result in any number of negative life consequences—relationship trouble, financial problems, job loss, declining emotional and physical health, loss of interest in previously enjoyable activities, and even arrest. Interestingly, as science continues to learn more about human neurobiology, these well-researched, widely acknowledged *substance* addictions are fast becoming just one part of what might constitute an *addictive disorder.*

Is There a New Definition for Addiction?

Until very recently, addiction and its treatment were viewed solely in terms of someone's problematic relationship to specific addictive substances. However, as we have gained research-based insight into how both substances and emotionally arousing behavioral patterns affect the human brain, the American Society of Addiction Medicine (ASAM) has moved to embrace a more inclusive definition of addiction. This encom-

< 133 >

passes not only drugs and alcohol, but also what addiction specialists call "process" or behavioral addictions. As of 2011, ASAM defines addiction in this way:

> Addiction is a primary, chronic disease of brain reward, motivation, memory, and related circuitry. Dysfunction in these circuits leads to characteristic biological, psychological, social, and spiritual manifestations. This is reflected in an individual pathologically pursuing reward and/or relief by substance use *and other behaviors* [emphasis added][1]

Note that ASAM's definition does not differentiate between being addicted to a substance, a behavior, or both. Of course, everything we ingest is a substance of some sort, and everything we do is a behavior of some sort. So it might seem as if just about anything can become an addiction. But this is not true. To qualify as having addictive potential, the behavior or substance must bring the user an experience of pleasure in some way. Addiction is further defined by the following symptoms:

- **Loss of control.** Addicts promise themselves and others that they will stop using the substance or engaging in their problem behavior—that they "won't do it again." They endlessly commit to change, but ultimately they are unable to *not do* the things they hope, try, promise, or want to discontinue.
- **Continued use despite significant adverse consequences.** Addicts get arrested, lose jobs, and have health, relationship, financial, and personal losses directly related to their addiction, but they return to use the substance or reengage in the behavior anyway.
- **Preoccupation to the point of obsession.** Over time, the driving force and primary focus of the addict's life becomes being involved with and using the pleasurable drug or behavior. Finding it, getting it, and doing it are always on the addict's mind, always a possibility, and always something the person will drop everything else to do.

< 134 >

Addicts also can develop a tolerance to both the substances and the behaviors they abuse. Over time, they have to either take more of their drug of choice or spend more time engaging in the addictive activity to achieve the same level of pleasure, distraction, or escape. Some addicts will escalate not only the amount, but also the level of intensity. For example, Sue, who had an online addiction to spending and shopping, talks about spending more and more time online as well as increasing how much money she spent and the number of goods she purchased. Addicts like Sue can also experience emotional cravings or even signs of physical withdrawal when they lose access to their substance or behavioral distraction of choice. Many technology-based activities such as accessing porn, online gambling, and video gaming, to name just a few, have addictive potential, as they evoke feelings of extreme pleasure and satisfaction while also serving as a source of profound, albeit momentary, distraction.

Technology Escalates Addiction

One fact that often seems to go unnoticed is that the problem of addiction—to both substances and behaviors—is now and always has been driven by human technological advances. Technology in all of its forms delivers an increasingly wide array of powerful substances and experiences that are, for some, emotionally, psychologically, and/or physically unmanageable.

This is not to say that some people don't have a genetic predisposition toward addiction. In fact, study after study shows a propensity for addiction and emotional vulnerability that is indeed hereditary. Alcoholism, for one, shows up in significantly higher rates in certain races, cultures, and families—strongly indicating genetic vulnerability. We also know that profound trauma in childhood or even later in life can also lead to addictive behavior.

Human technological advances can, however, increase the odds of actually developing an addiction. Consider the following substances and experiences listed in the charts on page 136, all made more accessible, affordable, and intense by human technological invention.

< 135 >

Analog Problems

How Substances + Technology = Increased Potential for Abuse*

Original Substance	Technological Process	Potential Problems
Tobacco leaves	Mass produced cigarettes	Nicotine addiction
Wheat/sugar	Inexpensive, high calorie, low nutrition snacks	Child/adult obesity
Coca leaves	Chemical refinement into rock and powder form	Cocaine addiction
Naturally occurring and man-made substances	Chemical refinement into prescription drugs	Methamphetamines, LSD, ecstasy, GHB, sedatives, stimulants, opiates, heroin

*Note how technology (via manufacturing and mass production techniques) has escalated both the intensity and distribution of the intensified substances.

Digital Problems

How Experiences + Technology = Increased Potential for Abuse*

Original Form	Technological or Digital Form	Potential Problems
Sexual imagery via drawings, storytelling and literature	Print, film, video and online porn	Porn addiction, relationship and sexual dysfunction
Gambling, gaming among friends or community	24/7 online gambling and gaming	Excessive gaming, gambling addiction
Shopping for goods/services	24/7 online spending, shopping, bidding	Spending and hoarding problems

*Note how technology (via digital, mobile and social media) has escalated both the intensity and inexpensive access to the intensified experiences.

< 136 >

Consider our nation's obesity epidemic. Would it be nearly as severe if not for the development and distribution of the inexpensive processed grains and refined sugars that now comprise so much of our diet? Those types of foods infest every mini-mart and gas station from Alaska to Miami. Prior to cheap mass distribution this problem simply did not exist.

Let's examine cocaine. Back in the days of yore, how many coca leaves did one have to chew while working in the fields to be considered a cocaine addict? The answer is, it didn't matter. Pure coca leaves produce only a mild stimulant effect, much like caffeine. It was virtually harmless. Yet once we were able to refine the plant and produce cocaine in the powder and rock forms commonly used today, a clearly visible problem arose.

What about distilling alcohol? Since almost the beginning of time humans have made and enjoyed wine, ale, and mead. In the 1870s we developed the technology to inexpensively distill spirits, resulting in high-alcohol-content "hard liquor" (whiskey, rum, vodka, gin), along with the ability to cheaply distribute it via the U.S. national railroad system. These advances in technology were the necessary prologue to the U.S. prohibition laws of the early twentieth century. As high-proof liquor became cheap to manufacture and distribute, the negative effects became more apparent. Suddenly a whole lot of people were exposed to a much more powerful (refined) version of the alcohol than they were used to consuming. Many were ill prepared to handle this more intense substance. Arguments, domestic violence, public brawling, and gunplay escalated exponentially in the late nineteenth century, directly related to alcohol abuse. And as the result, the United States banned liquor consumption entirely for nearly a decade.

Now let's consider porn. Can somebody really be addicted to it? It does seem highly unlikely that naked cave drawings and the *Kama Sutra* images (pre-photography, pre-film, pre-video) could have spawned too many sex addicts. Yet with today's highly refined, carefully manipulated, digitally transmitted, instantly accessible, and seemingly endless supply of porn, is it any wonder that some of the more emotionally vulnerable among us repeatedly turn to it for comfort, distraction, and emotional escape?

< 137 >

The following timeline outlines the pace at which humans have increasingly accessed sexual content over time. Note the escalating speed of access to increasingly stimulating forms of sexual content and experience.

Timeline of Human Access to Sexual Content and Contact

Prehistory to the 1860s	<ul><li>recreational and intimate sexuality</li><li>cave drawings and painted pornography</li><li>affairs and infidelity</li><li>public baths and steamrooms</li><li>prostitutes and harems</li><li>masturbation</li></ul>
1860s to 1970s	<ul><li>photographic porn</li><li>porn movies</li><li>porn theaters (XXX)</li></ul>
1970s to 1990s	<ul><li>video (VCR and BETA)</li><li>phone sex</li><li>softcore porn on cable TV</li><li>"adult" and "escort" sections in the yellow pages, magazines, and newspapers</li></ul>
1990s to 2004	<ul><li>BBS (online bulletin board systems)</li><li>websites for porn and prostitution</li><li>online porn and file transfer sites</li><li>chat rooms</li><li>online hookups (such as Craigslist)</li><li>webcams and interactive live sex</li></ul>
2004 to the present	<ul><li>sexting and live video streaming</li><li>smartphones with hookup apps</li><li>social networks (Facebook and Twitter)</li><li>virtual world sex (Second Life)</li><li>virtual sex environments</li><li>teledildonics</li><li>video chat and webcam sex</li></ul>

< 138 >

Processing the "Process" Addictions

As noted, Western culture is significantly less familiar with behavioral or process addictions than substance addictions. Even among therapist professionals there is still considerable confusion. This lack of understanding is in part due to the fact that many potentially addictive behaviors are for most people healthy, life-affirming activities that involve little concern or personal struggle. For example, recreational sex, Internet video gaming, and occasional online casino visits can be fun and enjoyable distractions for most, yet some people find themselves addicted to these same activities. Think of it another way: Most people who drink alcohol, even to the point of being drunk, can stop drinking whenever they wish. They are not addicted to alcohol. However, some people, once they start drinking, simply can't stop. They are alcoholics. Behavioral addicts are exactly the same, as they experience a different relationship with pleasurable activities such as sex, gambling, gaming, or eating than most people.

Eating and sexual activity—both potentially addictive behaviors—are interesting examples of potential process addictions. Each contributes to both individual survival and survival of the species, so our brains are programmed to encourage participation in these behaviors. These activities trigger a neurochemical response in the reward center of the brain, resulting in feelings of pleasure. Using alcohol and addictive drugs causes a similar response. In fact, almost all potentially addictive substances and behaviors trigger the same basic neurochemical pleasure response. We see this in fMRI (functional magnetic resonance imaging) studies of the brain, which clearly show that the neuroarousal patterns of someone who is abusing cocaine and someone who is sexually excited are virtually indistinguishable. In other words, the human brain reacts to sex in much the same way as it reacts to cocaine.

This biochemical pleasure process is a key to developing and maintaining both substance and behavioral addictions. Essentially, some people who struggle with underlying emotional or psychological issues can subconsciously learn over time to manipulate the brain's pleasure response by ingesting a particular substance or engaging in a certain activity in a misguided attempt to cope with stress and/or to distract

< 139 >

themselves from emotional pain. Repeatedly abusing a substance or behavior in this way can teach the brain that the way to feel better is to ingest more of that substance or engage in more of that behavior. No matter what the specific substance or behavior, the drive to abuse it is the same. Addicts want to feel better, which usually means feeling less. They have learned that turning to certain drugs or behaviors is the easiest way to temporarily disconnect, numb out, and experience pleasurable distractions in the midst of life's challenges.

Sadly, and despite overwhelming clinical evidence to the contrary, the general public often mistakenly views behavioral addictions as moral flaws and as less serious than substance addictions. Yet professionals who treat people with such addictions consistently witness the countless ways in which out-of-control impulsive, compulsive, and addictive relationships with food, spending, sex, gaming, gambling, and other behaviors wreak the same havoc on families, careers, and lives as addiction to drugs and alcohol.

The Triple-A Engine: Driving Online Addiction

With online behavioral addictions the "Triple-A Engine" of accessibility, affordability, and anonymity provided by the Internet and other forms of digital technology is the driving force.[2]

The Three "A's"

What has driven the most profound changes in our experience of information gathering and human contact over the past twenty years?

- access
- affordability
- anonymity

The theory behind these three "A's" is simple: the more readily any technology allows access to content and/or information, and the more affordable and anonymous that access is, the more people there are who will choose to access that material.

The tech-connect boom has dramatically increased the average person's ability to affordably and anonymously access endless quantities of

< 140 >

highly distracting, emotionally rewarding pleasurable games, material, and activities—everything from the Internet's 24/7 "shopping mall" to multiplayer video games, high-stakes gambling, highly graphic pornography, and casual sexual hookups. This *proliferation of access* is causing tremendous problems for many people with pre-existing addictive disorders, social inhibitions, impulsivity, early trauma, and attachment and mood disorders—all of which can contribute to long-term, profoundly harmful yet repetitive patterns of behavioral acting out.

As a result, addiction rears its ugly head. This is especially true when these substances or experiences are highly refined and amplified, as in the case of newer pharmaceutical drugs, gaming, and Internet porn. As our increasing technological interconnectivity has brought with it accessibility, affordability, and anonymity, addiction and mental health professionals are seeing a corresponding increase in the number of people struggling with tech-driven behavioral addictions.

Gambling Online

Among the most common tech-driven behavioral addictions is compulsive gambling, also called pathological gambling and gambling addiction. Compulsive gambling is an uncontrollable urge to gamble despite direct and profound negative consequences and a desire to quit. Typically, gambling addicts will play whatever game is available, but their preference is fast-paced games like video poker, slots, and roulette, where rounds end quickly and there is an immediate opportunity to play again. Digital technology can create a *huge* problem for gambling addicts, as they no longer need to travel to a casino, horse or dog track, or any other typical wagering venue. Instead, online gamblers can simply log onto a gambling website or smartphone app—from work, home, or even while on vacation—load some funds into their account, and then "lose themselves" for a while in the excitement of wagering.

For some, gambling can become a problem from the very first wager. More often, however, gambling addiction develops over time. With compulsive gambling, as is the case with most addictions, tolerance develops as the addiction progresses, so maintaining the same level of excitement requires larger and/or more frequent bets—often sums the

< 141 >

addict can't afford to lose. Complicating matters is the oft-occurring compulsion to keep playing in an effort to regain past losses. Consequently, many gambling addicts rack up tens or even hundreds of thousands of dollars in debt.

Consider the story of John, a forty-four-year-old real estate professional, now attending Gamblers Anonymous:

> Internet poker started out just like any other fun online game— with rewards, prizes, and other players who had some time to kill. It was a fun way to blow off some steam at the end of a tough day. But within three years, I had lost so much money that I had to mortgage my house and use my kid's college fund just to keep the family afloat. All of a sudden, it's not so fun anymore.

Those who start gambling in their teens are at much greater risk of developing a gambling problem than those who start gambling as adults.[3] This risk seems to be enhanced by digital natives' affinity for technology. In a review of 1,300 calls to the National Problem Gambling Helpline, 106 individuals (8 percent) reported that their primary problem was online gambling—and the predominant age of those individuals was eighteen to twenty-five.[4] Furthermore, a recent study conducted by the Annenberg Foundation found that nearly 600,000 American youth (ages fourteen to twenty-two) reported gambling on the Internet on a weekly basis.[5]

Not surprisingly, financial problems are the most obvious symptom of a gambling addiction. Compulsive gamblers can quickly deplete savings and credit lines, running up massive debt. They sometimes experience severe depression and suicidal thoughts directly related to their losses. They can also develop related problems with alcohol and drugs. Families of gambling addicts experience higher-than-average rates of domestic violence and child abuse. Children of gambling addicts are at greater risk of becoming depressed, experiencing behavioral problems, and developing an addiction of their own. Gambling addicts sometimes steal or embezzle from work, deal drugs, or engage in prostitution to

< 142 >

pay for their gambling. Many end up losing their families, their jobs, and even their freedom.

Digital and Online Gaming

Digital gaming addiction is the extreme use of computer and video games (games like Second Life, World of Warcraft, and Grand Theft Auto). Use escalates to the point that it interferes with daily life. Gaming addicts play compulsively, often isolating themselves for hours or even days from family and friends, focusing almost entirely on in-game achievements. These troubled people abuse gaming as a way to escape from real life in much the same way that alcoholics and drug addicts use their addictions as an escape. Young people—digital natives who've grown up with online gaming—are particularly at risk. Consider this experience, told by Jeff, a father in his late forties:

> Back in the late 1990s I thought the best thing I could do for
> my eldest boy, Max, was to get him engaged with computers
> as early as possible. I mean, that's the future, right? So as soon
> as his hands could hold them, I got him involved with the little
> kids' games that I'd buy at GameStop. Soon after it was digital
> pads, then interactive gaming on the laptop we bought him so
> he could do his schoolwork. I thought this was a good thing,
> and maybe for some kids it is. But the day Max's teacher called
> to tell me that he hadn't turned in homework or read an as-
> signment in weeks was the day I finally got it. All the time he'd
> been spending on the computer was rarely related to school at
> all; it was about running around fantasy worlds with packs of
> people I don't even know. So tell me, what do I do now, take it
> away from him at fifteen? It's not like a kid can do without a
> computer these days.

Some scholars have suggested that a strong social dependence on online gaming can arise when online interaction with other gamers becomes more important than real-world relationships.[6] After all, digital gaming often contains a predatory, pack-animal element that appeals to

< 143 >

CLOSER TOGETHER, FURTHER APART

a lot of people, especially young males. Others scholars feel that digital gaming addiction is, like most other addictions, based on enjoyment of the neurochemical rush that gaming can provide, while again offering distraction from life's uncomfortable emotions and stressors. Still others focus on the ways that digital gaming may fulfill our basic need for social connection, thereby keeping some younger people from actually learning the live, interactive social skills needed to negotiate successful adult friendships, romance, and work relationships.

Results from studies on the prevalence of digital gaming addiction are all over the board, but one thing is clear: younger individuals, digital natives who've grown up almost constantly exposed to this form of entertainment, are most at risk. Anecdotal evidence also suggests military veterans—especially those who've seen action in places like the Middle East and are used to the intense, heart-pounding terror of war—are also more likely than most to find themselves hooked on interactive video games, especially war-oriented games. Veterans also seem to be disproportionately at risk for becoming hooked on the intensity of pornography, an issue discussed later in this chapter. Consider the story of Edgar, a twenty-five-year-old Army veteran:

> When I got back stateside, I didn't know what to do with myself, especially as most of the courses I wanted to take at my local community college were already filled up. In Afghanistan my unit had been in the thick of the action for more than a year. I'd been shot at, nearly blown up, and watched a good friend lose his leg to a landmine. If I wanted to stay alive over there, and I did, I needed to be in a constant state of alertness, with adrenaline pumping 24/7. But back home there was no such excitement. Even hooking up with my old girlfriend seemed boring. I knew of Army buddies who'd started drinking heavily or getting high a lot when they got home, but I never was much on those things. So instead, I started gaming with my kid brother, mostly World of Warcraft but also some other games. He was still in high school, so he could only play after school and on weekends, and he had other things he liked to do too. But I had

all the time in the world. Before I knew it, I was playing for ten or twelve hours a day. I gained a ton of weight just sitting there gaming and eating fast food. Of course I didn't exercise at all, because I never wanted to miss out on an online "mission" or "battle." I finally saw there was a problem when I realized one day that I hadn't taken a shower or shaved in over a week. I had black circles under my eyes, and my skin looked as if I hadn't seen the sun in months. Clearly something was wrong.

Excessive online gaming often has many symptoms in common with alcoholism, drug addiction, and other behavioral addictions, along with a few "gaming-specific" issues such as becoming more concerned with in-game interactions than real-world interactions. Typically, gaming addicts play for at least two hours daily; often, they play four or five times that amount. They can neglect their personal hygiene and diet, gaining or losing significant weight because of their addiction. Their sleep patterns are disrupted, as they "lose themselves" in the games and forget about time. They avoid friends and family, fail to meet their obligations, and slowly lose interest in activities they used to enjoy, such as going out with friends, participating in team sports, and spending time on other hobbies. In one extreme instance it was reported that a seventeen-year-old boy was playing for up to fifteen hours at a time, skipping meals and only stopping when he blacked out.[7]

Online Shopping and Spending Addiction

The psychological term for spending addiction is oniomania. The word aptly derives from *onios*, the Greek word meaning "for sale," combined with *mania*, meaning "madness." The disorder is also referred to as a compulsive spending, shopping addiction, and compulsive buying disorder. Compulsive spenders shop obsessively despite the damage this does to their finances and even their relationships. Oftentimes they try to cut back or quit, but can't. The primary difference between normal shoppers and compulsive spenders is that compulsive spenders consistently use shopping as a way to escape life stressors and uncomfortable emotions. For them, the act of shopping is a way to avoid their day-to-

< 145 >

day problems. In other words, compulsive spenders shop relentlessly because they want to feel better (that is, feel less). Typically such people suffer from unresolved early life trauma or another underlying psychological disorder such as social anxiety, obsessive compulsive disorder, depression, or low self-esteem—the same basic conditions that lead to other addictions. Shopping becomes a way to self-regulate emotions and dissociate from life. Consider the experience of Suzanne, a fifty-four-year-old divorced legal secretary:

> First I got into Overstock.com, then Gilt, then Net-A-Porter, and now it's like a shopping free-for-all. Not too long ago I was pretty good at making and keeping a budget. But since my kids left for school and I'm less busy, it seems like the boxes just stack up outside my apartment door while I just go on buying. I often buy stuff I don't need; sometimes I return it and sometimes I just put it away and try not to think about it anymore. I know that this is all going to catch up to me pretty soon, and not in a good way. But once I get online I don't seem able to avoid spending even though I've promised myself to stop.

Certainly websites and apps such as those created by eBay, Amazon, and Groupon play into the American dream of feathering one's nest with baubles, gadgets, and whatever else it is that catches one's eye. And there is no doubt that digital technology, with its 24/7 access to goods and its consistently stimulating, constantly changing shopping environments, facilitates this process. That doesn't, however, mean we are a nation of shopaholics. The vast majority of digital shoppers purchase items they both want and need—things that used to require getting in the car and driving to an actual store to purchase. In other words, they're not spending money on anything they wouldn't normally buy; they're just making their purchases in a slightly different way.

People addicted to spending and online shopping, on the other hand, will often buy things they neither want nor care about once the transaction is complete. Female shopping addicts hang new clothes in the closet without even removing the tags. Men stash fancy electron-

< 146 >

ic toys, unopened, on shelves in their garage. In other words, compulsive spending isn't about buying items the shopper needs or even desires; it's about temporarily escaping the discomfort of day-to-day life through the "rush" of spending and/or "getting the best deal" on that momentarily desired shiny object.

For compulsive spenders, one out-of-control shopping spree is never enough. Neighborhood malls and Internet shopping sites are beacons that pull them in like moths to a flame—they just can't stay away. Throughout the year, they purchase and give expensive gifts, not because they are filled with love or moved to celebrate a birthday or holiday, but because they need an excuse to spend. Compulsive spenders lie about and cover up their behavior by hiding purchased goods, price tags, and receipts. Some even destroy new purchases in an attempt to conceal their spending. They also learn to shop in secret. Digital technology aids and abets them in this endeavor, allowing them to avoid malls and other bricks-and-mortar stores where friends or family members might spot them making unnecessary purchases. The finances of compulsive spenders are nearly always strained.

On the surface, it can seem difficult to distinguish between an addictive spender and a normal shopper. Spending addicts typically experience a rush of excitement before shopping, a deep sense of pleasure and gratification while shopping, and a loss of excitement coupled with guilt, shame, and remorse after shopping. But who among us has not had those same feelings after anticipating, shopping for, and buying an overly indulgent item? However, non-compulsive spenders laugh it off and if necessary return the unwanted items, no harm done, whereas compulsive spenders hide their behavior and suffer through intense feelings of guilt, shame, and remorse. And what do they do to help relieve these feelings? What else? They self-medicate with *yet another round of compulsive spending*. This is the face of behavioral addiction.

Sadly, what compulsive spenders are actually attempting to purchase is peace. Like all of us, they want to feel connected, appreciated, and admired, rather than depressed, self-hating, and anxious. Yet it doesn't matter how much money they have or how successful they are—all the "stuff" in the world can't fill the emptiness they feel inside.

< 147 >

Sex Addiction: Not as Much Fun as It Sounds...

Also known as hypersexuality or sexual compulsion, sexual addiction is a dysfunctional preoccupation with sexual fantasy and behavior. It often involves the obsessive pursuit of non-intimate sex, pornography, compulsive masturbation, romantic intensity, and objectified partner sex. Online porn addiction, with or without masturbation, is now the most prevalent form of sex addiction. Today nearly all forms of sex addiction, including porn addiction, are technology driven—everything from porn and dating websites to webcams to casual sex hookup apps.

Interestingly, sex addicts are not hooked on the act of sex, per se. Rather, they are hooked on the neurochemical high evoked by their intense sexual fantasy life and related ritualistic behaviors. Sex addicts can and do spend hours, sometimes even days, in this elevated, trance-like state—high on the search for sex—without actually engaging in a sexual act. As such, sex and porn addicts typically spend more time engaged in the pursuit of sex than in the actual sex act. They abuse their personal neurochemistry in the same way that alcoholics and drug addicts abuse alcohol, heroin, and cocaine.

As the addiction progresses, sex addicts begin to organize their lives around the pursuit of sexual activity (with self or others), spending inordinate amounts of time viewing and masturbating to porn, or planning, pursuing, and engaging in casual, anonymous, or paid sexual encounters. At the same time, like all addicts, they increasingly neglect important relationships, interests, and both work and personal responsibilities. And when the acting out ends, they experience overwhelming feelings of guilt, shame, and remorse. As is typical of addiction in general, some sex addicts will try to quit or limit their addictive behavior—especially following a directly related negative consequence (arrest, threat of divorce, and so on)—but on their own they are rarely successful. As time passes, they act out more frequently, for longer periods of time, and often progress to more intense and/or bizarre sexual interests. For addicts, sexual acting out takes place regardless of their outward success, intelligence, physical attractiveness, and existing intimate relationships. Consider, for example, the experience of Jack. This thirty-seven-year-old father of three explains what his addiction is like:

< 148 >

I don't know if I'm addicted to online porn or what, but I do know that I spend *at least* two to three hours daily on porn and sex hookup sites. During a few of these late-night sessions, I even called a few online escort services, with my wife in bed in the very next room. It worries me that one of these days I'm going to go from looking up to hooking up. And this is time I could be spending with my family, resting, or even catching up on work. But these days my computer feels like some kind of siren that calls out to me every time I walk by. And more often than not, I put aside and risk all that I hold dear to answer that call.

Digital technology has played a huge role in the development and maintenance of sexual addiction. Porn addicts are especially vulnerable to the lure of digital technology and the seemingly endless array of sexual and romantic stimulation it provides. Research suggests that cyber-porn addicts can spend *at least* eleven or twelve hours per week online viewing porn—sometimes double or even triple that amount, depending on the addict's state of mind. If the addict is also a compulsive masturbator, that time is simultaneously spent in self-stimulation. This behavior can occasionally be coupled with drug use, most often stimulants such as cocaine or crystal meth and sexual enhancement drugs like Viagra and Cialis.

Love: The Many-Splendored Addiction

Closely related to sex addiction is the concept of love addiction, a compulsive search for romantic attachment as a way of dissociating from and/or self-medicating uncomfortable emotions and underlying psychological conditions. The obsessive search for love is today almost wholly located within the world of digital technology. Dating sites, "romantic" chat rooms (both text and video), apps, and even social media sites can fan the flames of compulsive "love" relationships. Social media sites in particular have become a new and socially acceptable place to peruse intimate photos, gain personal information, seek out hot chats, and hook up for virtual or in-person encounters. Love addicts increas-

< 149 >

ingly describe these networks as a *primary location* in which they "lose themselves" in their obsessive search for romantic intensity.

For love addicts, romance, sexuality, and emotional closeness are experiences more often beset with painful emotional highs and lows than gifted with real intimacy or love. Living in a chaotic, sometimes desperate world of need and emotional despair, fearful of being alone or being rejected, the love addict endlessly longs for that special relationship, the one that he or she believes will make him or her feel complete. Love addicts live in fear of never finding that special someone or, even worse, meeting that person only to be found lacking and unworthy of the person's love and affection. They spend their lives focused on the search for sexual and romantic partners in every situation. JoAnne, a single banker in her late twenties, describes her struggle with love addiction:

> Eventually I began to hide my dates. I didn't want my friends to know that I'd met someone new because so many times in the past I'd said, "He's the one," and then it hadn't worked out. I thought they would laugh at me if I brought yet another guy to the table. In desperation I tried blind dates, speed dating, chat rooms, virtual dating, and dating websites. I had profiles on Match.com, eHarmony, and three or four others. I even put up a profile on JDate, ignoring the fact that I'm not Jewish. Over time, my life became more and more about searching online for the right guy and less and less about enjoying my "real" life and doing the things that make me happy.

Essentially, love addicts are attracted to the same type and level of emotional/neurochemical intensity as sex addicts, and they are usually just as detached from the reality of their situation and its costs to their lives. For them, the search for that special person becomes the sole object of their focus and needs, often to the exclusion of outside interests and support. Like any sex addict—who gives up time, health, money, self-esteem, and more in the pursuit of feeling high—love addicts neglect personal interests, hobbies, exercise, self-care, and jobs to devote

< 150 >

more time and energy to finding and/or maintaining an idealized partnership. They search for love on dating sites and social media, posting about it, tweeting about it, and texting and sexting like mad to hook and/or keep their "perfect partner."

Social Media Obsession

Social media can be problematic even for people not addicted to sex or love. Many people "lose themselves" in an obsessive quest to have the most "friends" or followers, to have their lovingly constructed posts and tweets responded to in positive ways, or to "look the best" in the online universe by posting incessantly about whatever it is they are doing and how wonderful their life is. Thus social media, an entirely digital phenomenon, can become an addiction unto itself and a quick and easy substitute for true self-esteem, real-world relationships, and genuine intimate connection.

Cross- and Co-Occurring Addictive Disorders

People who are cross-addicted switch from one addiction to another, whereas people with co-occurring addictions struggle with multiple addictions at the same time. Cross- and co-occurring disorders are quite common among all types of addicts, both substance and behavioral. Here are a few common cross- and co-occurring addiction scenarios:

- After leaving treatment for an eating disorder, Lori, a divorced fifty-one-year-old who had never been interested in online gaming, discovered Second Life, playing it as many as forty hours per week—in essence, replacing her binge and purge cycle with another addiction, online "alternate reality" games.
- After attending Alcoholics Anonymous meetings daily and remaining sober from alcohol for three months, Raymond, age sixty-seven, started shopping online. At first he bought items he needed or gifts for his wife. Before long, however, he was buying things he neither needed nor wanted, running up huge amounts of credit card debt.

< 151 >

Battling cross- and co-occurring addictions can sometimes feel like playing a game of Whac-a-mole, the carnival game where you pound down plastic moles whenever and wherever they pop up, only to immediately spot various other moles rising up from their holes.[8] No matter how many moles you hammer down, another one seems to appear. Addictions can be the same. One addiction pops up, and while you're busy pounding it down, another addiction emerges.

Obsession or Addiction?

Nearly everyone can *look* addicted at various points in life. For instance, virtually everyone has experienced the "rush" of first love—those days, weeks, or months when how the other person looks, walks, talks, eats, and thinks is the subject of endless fantasy, excitement, and late-night chats. This obsessive period is the fodder of romantic songs and greeting cards everywhere. Most people either innately know or learn through experience that this wonderful time is a temporary state, that this romantic intensity is the catalyst that brings about the bonding necessary to sustain long-term love and attachment, but it is not in and of itself long-term love and attachment. Life in the digital universe is similar; certain things seem great for a while and we seem a bit obsessed, but most of the time those things eventually either get boring or morph into something more meaningful.

These periods of infatuation are routinely experienced by all people, both online and off. People with kids know this well. For your son, his Bob the Builder phase turns into an infatuation with Transformers, which turns into rabidly following *Star Wars*, then the Cincinnati Reds, and eventually to hours and hours of Xbox. That same son might later discover digital pornography. But if he's like most boys he will eventually find both online gaming and porn two-dimensional and unfulfilling, and he will long for personal contact, real-world friendships, and in-the-flesh intimate interaction. He will eventually want to have a more connected experience, and his online interactions will naturally diminish. These periods of childhood/adolescent infatuation typically continue into adulthood, with some activities becoming healthy hobbies, such as going to the gym, and others simply fading away.

< 152 >

Even for people addicted to digital technology, the news is not all bad. Today, people who recognize they are using digital technology compulsively to escape life's challenges can seek and readily find help. Information and resources for recovering from technology driven addictions are located in Appendix II.

< 153 >

CHAPTER SEVEN

What's Coming Next Has Already Been

When one door closes, another door opens; but we so often look so long and regretfully upon the closed door, that we do not see the ones which open for us.
—Alexander Graham Bell, American inventor 1847–1922

In the late 1980s and early 1990s, Milli Vanilli topped the pop music charts with their debut album, *Girl You Know It's True*, even winning a Grammy Award for Best New Artist. Shortly thereafter, fame turned to infamy when it was revealed that neither of the two singers had voiced the lead vocals on their hit record. Milli Vanilli was fake, and the world was incensed! So much so that the Grammy people actually took their award back. Adios Milli Vanilli!

My, how things have changed. On January 21, 2013, at Barack Obama's second U.S. presidential inauguration, millions watched pop star Beyoncé sing our national anthem accompanied by a live orchestra—but what we saw and what we heard were not the same thing. As it turns out, Beyoncé's voice and the orchestra were mostly muted, with a studio version of the anthem pumped out to cover any potential imperfections in the "live" performance. Well, a lot of people noticed, but few seemed to really care. After all, it was 30 degrees outside—notoriously bad singing weather. Beyoncé wanted to sound her best, so she chose to present a partly live but mostly studio version of our national anthem. A few days later, at a press conference for the 2013 Super Bowl (she was the halftime entertainment), Beyoncé stated, "I am a perfectionist, and … I did not have time to rehearse with the orchestra. It was a live television show and a very, very important emotional show for me, one of my

< 155 >

proudest moments. Due to no proper sound-check, I did not feel comfortable taking a risk. It was about the President and the inauguration and I wanted to make him and my country proud, so I decided to sing along with my prerecorded track, which is very common in the music industry."[1] She then went on to blithely hype her upcoming concert tour.

In 2013, Beyoncé's inaugural "deception" caused hardly a ripple of discontent. And it is worth noting her statement about artists singing along to prerecorded tracks being "very common in the music industry" these days. That statement was quite factual. Modern pop concerts today are huge productions featuring not just music and lights but pyrotechnics, hydraulics, dozens of costume changes, and endless high-energy dance numbers. In such shows performers *have* to lip-sync, at least part of the time. It is simply not possible to put that much energy into dancing, prancing, and morphing into various looks while smiling and waving and, at the same time, belting out a tune. It doesn't matter how good your voice is or how physically in shape the artist, it simply can't be done. If you don't believe this, try singing along to the music in your favorite exercise video while also doing the exercise. Because of this escalating demand for pop artists to create larger and more elaborate shows, performers now routinely lip-sync to their (oftentimes digitally "sweetened") prerecorded music, and nobody seems to mind too much. The days of Milli Vanilli outrage appear to be far behind us.

Walking the New Line Between Reality and Fantasy

As digital technology advances, the line between fantasy and reality becomes increasingly blurry. And not just in the music industry. For example, consider all those alluring, perfect magazine cover faces and bodies, visually screaming for attention, lined up one after another in the grocery store checkout aisle. Is it really a surprise to anyone that 99.9 percent of the time those perfect teeth, that luxurious hair, and all those carefully toned muscles have had more than just a few digital tweaks? We all know it's fake, right? But we buy the stuff anyway ... and in droves!

And let's get R-E-A-L about "reality" TV. When you watch a reality television show, the drama unfolding in front of you is about as far

< 156 >

from "unscripted" as the endless commercials that we now tend to skip rather than endure. MSN commentator Ted Anthony sums it up, "In America these days, in countless tiny ways, much of what we see and experience isn't exactly what it seems. We know it, too. And often we don't care because what we're getting just seems to 'pop' more than its garden-variety, without-the-special-sauce counterpart."[2] Anthony cites numerous examples of techno-trickery in his article, everything from digital photo retouching to "dramatized" modern journalism to the use of banned performance-enhancing drugs (PEDs) by athletes. About digital photography, he writes:

> The tools of artifice, once accessible only to professionals, have gone democratic. Now manipulators by the millions can erase blemishes, unwanted features and entire people. With the tap of a smartphone touchscreen, you can make an image taken seconds ago look like a "vintage" snapshot from a 1972 Polaroid or a 19th century tintype. A few years back, HP even came out with a camera that had a "slimming feature," allowing you to choose just how much girth you wanted to remove for Facebook or the family album.[3]

Let's face it. We now live in a world in which *fake is the new real*. Is it any wonder, then, that those more comfortable and familiar with life in the digital universe can feel as if they are having a relationship with someone they've never met *in person* (or who may not even exist in the real world)? Or that the emotions stirred up by a virtual relationship can feel every bit as powerful and fulfilling as those evoked by a traditional in-the-flesh interaction, and can be every bit as painful when the "relationship" ends. Our music (Beyoncé and others), entertainment (reality television shows), sports heroes (Lance Armstrong, among many), and, increasingly, our romantic and sexual encounters are nearly all technologically enhanced to enrapture, mesmerize, and enthrall us, techno-designed to increase enjoyment while guaranteeing satisfaction. Okay, sometimes we get angry when we discover we've been duped, but more and more often we are too busy and distracted to complain. So Honey

< 157 >

Boo Boo as some kind of low-rent Shirley Temple inexplicably manages to entertain us, and, contrived or not, the enjoyment we receive seems to be all that matters.

Digital natives, increasingly raised half in the real world and half in the digital universe, seem less and less concerned than past generations about this type of deception, even embracing the craft and technology used to create these consistent illusions. Moreover, younger people seem to view this well-done sleight of hand, when juxtaposed against their IRL experience, as two parts of the same reality. Meanwhile, older generations, perhaps longing to find something they believe to be *real* submerged within all this pretense, express great concern that their children and grandchildren are unable to distinguish between reality and fantasy. Yet overall it seems that those perceptions and fears are very much of their generation. As we have seen throughout this book, perceptions and fears—in other words, *reality*—can change and evolve as time passes and new technologies are introduced. What one generation decries as "fake" and unworthy, another generation accepts and even adores. Who is right? Who is wrong? Who gets to decide?

Are You Real? Does It Matter?

Some will point to the Manti Te'o "scandal" that broke in early 2013 as further evidence against this blurring of what defines real versus what is online. The University of Notre Dame football star "fell in love" with a woman he'd met online who, in reality, was an emotionally disturbed young man posing online as a woman. Interestingly enough, according to Te'o, the thing he regretted most about this entire situation, after all was said and done, was that he had lied to his father by telling him he'd actually met this woman in person. Folks scratch their heads, wondering why this otherwise upstanding young man would tell such a lie to his loving, trusting father. Many digital natives, however, seem to understand that Te'o likely lied because he knew his older father would struggle to understand the depth of feeling he'd developed for a woman he'd met only in the digital universe.

And there's the rub. For digital natives, their social media interactions *feel every bit as real* and meaningful as meeting with someone in

< 158 >

person. And who's to say that they are wrong to feel what they feel? Even though his virtual paramour was not in fact a real person, the feelings Manti Te'o had for "her" were quite real. And the feelings that other young people now express toward their online digi-lovers and friends are often equally real. So yes, the occasional unscrupulous individual can use digital technology and the real life emotions it can evoke to scam and otherwise take advantage of trusting people, but it's not as if this is a new behavior. Romantic scams have occurred since the dawn of time, both with and without the use of technology. Shakespeare made quite a name for himself writing about very similar situations back in the sixteenth century! Yes, this is the type of story that digital immigrants fear, but blaming digital technology for the situation is misguided. Troubled people misbehave, and innocent people are sometimes victimized—with *and without* the Internet.

Digital Deprivation

Research recently conducted at the University of Maryland asked 200 random students to avoid using all digital media for twenty-four hours.[4] The following day they wrote about their experiences. One of the most common responses was the students' desire to be reconnected—to people, music, entertainment, news—*now*. They wanted instant gratification, primarily that which their smartphones provided 24/7. Without them, they felt bereft. Most thought they could give up television and the newspaper, but they couldn't live without their phones.

Many of the students used literal terms of addiction and withdrawal to describe their dependence on technology. One wrote of feeling isolated and lonely, followed by what might easily qualify as withdrawal symptoms. "By 2 p.m. I began to feel the urgent need to check my email, and even thought of a million ideas why I had to. I began to fidget, as if I was addicted to my iPod and other media devices, and maybe I am." Another student wrote, more succinctly, "I am clearly addicted and the dependency is sickening."[5]

But what if these students aren't addicted to technology per se, but rather to the very healthy and normal human desire for connection with others? What if their "dependence" on their smartphones and other

< 159 >

digital devices is actually evidence that they have successfully adapted to the ever-changing world by learning to meet their needs for inter-connectivity through use of the most constantly connected device they know? If that is the case, then the "problem" is not with them. They are not the ones in need of a reboot. Instead, it is the rest of us who need to adjust, accepting that these young people are now a step ahead of us on the evolutionary food chain. What if the *unproven idea* that young people, in their relationships to their phones, tablets, and other gadgets are somehow doing damage to themselves and to humanity is an idea formed by digital immigrants who don't know technology the way dig-ital natives do and, therefore, tend to fear and judge it?

Consider, as one such example, the words of Oxford University neuroscientist, writer, and broadcaster, Susan Greenfield (a digital im-migrant):

> Human identity, the idea that defines each and every one of us, could be facing an unprecedented crisis. It is a crisis that would threaten long-held notions of who we are, what we do, and how we behave. It goes right to the heart—or the head—of us all. This crisis could reshape how we interact with each other, alter what makes us happy, and modify our capacity for reaching our full potential as individuals. And it's caused by one simple fact: the human brain, that most sensitive of organs, is under threat from the modern world.[6]

Like Greenfield, many people view the Internet and other forms of digital technology as a threat. But perhaps these people are simply not able to absorb the many obvious advantages of technological progress—and without doubt there are benefits. For example, Greenfield's own research is focused primarily on understanding and ultimately finding a cure for Alzheimer's disease. Most people would be hard-pressed to find a downside to a *technologically sourced* cure for Alzheimer's. Such an advance would, indisputably, be changing humanity—indeed, the human brain—for the better. And such a cure actually seems inevitable, given what we now know about the brain's malleable nature.

< 160 >

Unfortunately, this malleability has a definite potential downside. The brain is shaped, not just metaphorically but physically, by a person's thoughts, activities, and environment. Currently, human beings, particularly young people, are experiencing an ever-increasing deluge of digital technologies—the Internet, social media, smartphones, apps, MP3s and MP4s, video games, virtual worlds, 3D and ultra-high-def televisions, and more—with newer options hitting the market every day. All of which, as Greenfield so eloquently writes, "have an impact on the micro-cellular structure and complex biochemistry of our brains. And that, in turn, affects our personality, our behavior and our characteristics."[7] In short, the technology of the modern world is most certainly altering our human identity. The humans of tomorrow will be very different from the humans of today in terms of their goals, their desires, the ways they learn and think, and, perhaps most importantly, their ability to care for and form intimate relationships with others. But what will that difference mean?

Tech Backlash

A common perception is that all young people love technology and interact with it constantly. And why wouldn't we think this? Let's face it, it's common to see kids walking down the street while tapping away at a smartphone—texting, tweeting, surfing the Internet, gaming, listening to music, watching YouTube, or whatever else it is that kids do. And if you see a group of young people hanging out together, they are probably as involved with their digital devices as they are with each other.

Interestingly enough, not all digital natives are as captivated by technology as you might think. For starters, there is the growing NoFap movement in which young males are choosing to not masturbate. Essentially, the movement is a reaction to the fact that some guys are losing interest in both finding and engaging with real-world sex partners thanks to the accessibility of digital pornography. The NoFap movement appears to be less about not masturbating than it is about rebelling against tech-sex. While digital technology has made their lives easier and more efficient, it has simultaneously left them feeling increasingly detached from meaningful, real-time human connections.

< 161 >

Some are eschewing digital interactions altogether, joining peer groups who are consciously choosing to put down their devices, thereby giving up on Facebook, Twitter, Instagram, and other social media sites. This digital native tech backlash is also evident in pop culture, appearing as a theme in numerous novels and movies, most notably *The Hunger Games*, in which "The Capitol" uses technology to control and sometimes even torment the population. Even advertisers are catching on, albeit slowly. In one recent television commercial a young professional is shown walking down the street, studiously engaged with his smartphone. As he taps at his phone, "digital people" pop up to remind him about meetings for work, necessary car repairs, getting his dry cleaning, and other tasks. Finally he enters a bar, sees his friends, puts his smartphone away, orders a beer, and starts to have a good time. The message provided here is it's important to disengage and relax in real time with real people.

Some young people like to express their individuality by studiously avoiding looking or being anything like their parents or grandparents. So when grandpa got his very own iPhone, suddenly it wasn't as cool as it once was, and when Grandma goes onto your Facebook page or follows you on Twitter or Pinterest, social media loses its appeal. So what are we to make of those "back to our roots" young men and women now choosing to reject the evolving digital world? While there will always be those who prefer the analog world to the digital, technology changes too quickly now to ever really go out of style. There is always something new. But some people are demonstrating that even though new things can easily capture and captivate, they may only do so for a short while. Eventually that glittering new device becomes a thing of the past. When that occurs, we tend to integrate it into our lives in a less obsessive manner, picking it up and using it occasionally, or we move onto something fresher and shinier.

This "moving on" process has already begun for some digital natives in relation to some all-consuming technologies like digital porn and social media. That doesn't mean that any of these technologies are going to disappear any time soon. In fact it's more likely that for some folks today, *avoiding tech is the trendy thing to do* while embracing it is to

< 162 >

join the pack. Hail individuality for all, but it seems obvious that tech is here to stay.

Opinions Aside, the Future Is Unknown

Consider a typical adult middle or upper class woman in the United States today. This is a woman who desires to work full time in a stimulating career that allows her to earn as much as a man, a woman who expects to be educated in a college where she is equal to the male students, a woman who daily drops off her two- and four-year-old children to be kept safe by paid caregivers in order to enter the larger world and achieve her full intellectual and professional potential. Less than 100 years ago, this modern American woman would have been considered at best a disgrace to her sex and, at worst, crazy. Yet today this is the likely path for the majority of motivated women. Are these changes any less reflective of human social and biological evolution than our children chatting online with friends after school as opposed to "going outside to play" as their parents once did? And what about fifty years from now? In light of the currently alarming acceleration of climate change, maybe the best place for our future children to spend time will be indoors in a well-oxygenated, climate-controlled home, connecting to others via a digital device. What if instead of destroying the human race, our relationship with technology ends up saving us? All possible. All unknown.

What we do know right now is that older generations tend to look upon the technologies and experiences of younger people with fear and concern. In the same way that parents of baby boomers feared that "sex, drugs, long hair, and rock and roll" were sowing the seeds of inhumanity, social chaos, and cultural doom, the parents of today worry about how younger people are communicating, interacting, and connecting. Perhaps, as suggested earlier, these concerns evolve out of the underlying fear shared by anyone old enough to recognize their own mortality that, without the attention and support of younger people, the older generation could be left to age and die alone. Rather than judging digital immigrants as inflexible and crotchety with age, perhaps a kinder way to view their fear and judgment of the digital generation would be as an expression of concern that they themselves will end up being pushed

< 163 >

aside by all these new distractions at the very time they become the most vulnerable.

We fear what we do not know. For instance, in the 1970s parents and the U.S. government feared that violence on television would produce a more violent culture; Senate hearings were even conducted. As it turns out, people who "grew up" with TV now live in a less violent society than the generation before. In a similar fashion, many of today's parents (and government agencies) now express fear that children's exposure to video game violence will produce a generation of violent adults; Senate hearings have again been convened. What will come to pass? Only time will tell.

The authors of this book believe that digital technology and all that has come with it is providing us with an opportunity to literally witness the human evolutionary process *in real time*. Through our observations of younger people and their relationship with technology, we can actually see the good, the bad, and the ugly of evolution. Undoubtedly today—for better or worse—human evolution and technological evolution are inextricably linked, and there is no turning back. If you don't believe it, just look around. The young people who had digital technology in their hands before they could eat strained fruit now walk, talk, laugh, love, and text all at the same time.

As is always the case with evolution, some individuals will do a better job of adapting than others. In the Stone Age, those who learned to use tools such as flints and spears flourished, while their less adaptable counterparts struggled to survive. Similarly, individuals who learn to use digital technology in healthy, productive ways are likely to thrive, and those who don't, won't. Here, as always, evolution favors those who adapt quickly and efficiently, and it weeds out those who do not. The only real difference between the Stone Age and the Digital Age is the speed at which we must now learn to acclimate ... or not.

Where Are We Now? Where Are We Going?

Any technology or experience that universally affects the ways in which we communicate and interact is bound to also affect the ways in which we love, relate, and build community. For instance, the wheel enhanced

< 164 >

our ability to get from place to place, widening our circle of potential partners. Another technological advance, written language, allowed us to "pitch woo" from afar via letter—an ability that has been repeatedly enhanced by technologies such as the telegraph, the telephone, the Internet, and most recently by the advent of smartphones and social media. So even though many digital immigrants might feel as if recent advances in technology are tolling a death-like knell for humanity, their far-more-digitally-accomplished children and grandkids would most likely wholeheartedly disagree. Some older digital immigrants fret that younger people, due to their consistent online interaction, are not able to learn the intricacies of embracing and tolerating an actual, real-world partner's needs, emotions, rejections, and criticisms. Meanwhile, others might argue, and just as validly, that young people are even better than their predecessors at forming communities, sharing information, finding people who share their interests, and interacting in general. Frankly, we don't know which of these arguments holds water. It doesn't really matter because that ship has already sailed—online.

< 165 >

AFTERWORD

This is a 100 percent true story. After a recent well attended clinical presentation that fully reflected the themes offered here in *Closer Together, Further Apart*, I was as usual greeted by a line of clinical psychotherapists waiting patiently to question, comment upon, and/or share their thoughts about its content.

One young clinician of twenty-eight years or so, clearly excited to have a moment with the speaker, said to me, "Thank you so much! I have been listening for the past three years as one speaker after another gave elaborate reasons why technological advances were bringing about the end of empathy, meaning, and relationships. Thank you for *not* being that voice once again, because it's simply not true and tech is what my generation is all about.

The very next woman in line was a warm, clearly empathic social worker in her late fifties who told me she had dedicated her life to educating the underserved. Looking into my eyes knowingly, she said, "Thank you for the talk. I think I have a much better understanding now of how technology is affecting us. But maybe you don't quite understand that the kids I teach don't seem to know how to relate. All they seem to do is sit in front of their screens doing lord knows what. Now you can't tell me that's good for them?"

And so it goes ...

Rob Weiss

Robert Weiss, LCSW, December 6, 2013

< 167 >

APPENDIX I

Online Protection for Children: Tracking, Filtering, and Software Options

Digital interconnectivity provides endless opportunities that support our very human needs for community and social interaction. Unfortunately, this increasing connectivity also brings easy access to a seemingly endless collection of imagery, information, and individuals—material and interactions from which you might like to protect your children. Happily, there are numerous "parental control" software programs that can help shield children from online dangers. Parents should look for the following in any protective software:

- **Customizable controls:** First and foremost, the software should include a customizable Internet filter. Most products offer various preset filtering levels, filtering out more material for younger children than for older children. The best products allow for the blacklisting and whitelisting of certain sites—meaning that sites normally allowed at a certain preset filtering level can be manually blocked (blacklisted), and sites normally blocked can be manually unblocked (whitelisted).

- **Accountability:** The software should include some sort of accountability function, meaning you are notified of the child's online travels. The accountability feature should be customizable, allowing you to receive daily reports, weekly reports, monthly reports, on-demand reports, and even instant notification if your child uses or attempts to use

< 169 >

the Internet in a certain way. Ideally, the software should allow for more than one accountability partner so that both parents receive these reports.

- **HTTPS and proxy blocking:** Tech-savvy children have been known to use proxies (intermediary web servers) and encrypted HTTPS connections to circumvent filtering software. The software should prevent such abuses and be impossible to uninstall without a password. Ideally, the program will notify you if your child attempts to uninstall or circumvent the filtering and accountability features of the program.

- **Ease of use:** The software should be easy to install and to customize. If you are protecting more than one device, you should be able to configure global settings using a web-based interface. In this way, you can establish settings on all of your child's devices simultaneously instead of dealing with each machine individually.

- **Availability for your device and use on multiple devices:** Always check the software publisher's website to make sure their product is appropriate for your computer, laptop, smartphone, and other mobile devices. It doesn't matter how great a program's features are if it doesn't function on your equipment. Also check to see how many and what types of devices the license covers. Most children need protection on a home computer, a laptop, and a smartphone.

Even the best Internet filtering software is not perfect. Parental control software programs should not be viewed as *parental enforcers*, but rather as *tools of parenting* that can help you to protect your child (through the filtering features) and to build trust with your child (through the accountability features). At the time of this writing, the best filtering/ accountability programs include:

- Bsecure Family Safety, www.bsecure.com
- CovenantEyes, www.covenanteyes.com

< 170 >

- McAfee Safe Eyes and McAfee Family Protection, www.mcafee.com/us
- Net Nanny, www.netnanny.com

Reviews that are updated regularly can be found at www. sexualrecovery.com/protecting-children-teens-online-porn.php.

< 171 >

APPENDIX II

Resources

Compulsive Gambling Resources
General Information
- Helpguide.org offers great information about compulsive gambling—what it is, how to recognize it, how it can be treated, and so on. Their website is www. helpguide.org.

Books
- H. Shaffer, *Change Your Gambling, Change Your Life: Strategies for Managing Your Gambling and Improving Your Finances, Relationships, and Health*. (Hoboken, NJ: Jossey-Bass, 2012).
- M. Lancelot, *Gripped by Gambling*. (Tucson, AZ: Wheatmark, 2007).
- R. Ladouceur and S. Lachance, *Overcoming Your Pathological Gambling: Workbook*. (NY: Oxford University Press 2006).

Twelve Step Groups
- Gamblers Anonymous, 213-386-8789, www.gamblersanonymous.org

Compulsive Spending Resources
General Information
- Useful information and links can be found at www.indiana. edu/~engs/hints/shop.html.

< 173 >

Books

- S. Palaian, *Spent: Break the Buying Obsession and Discover Your True Worth*. (Center City, MN: Hazelden, 2009).
- A. Benson, *To Buy or Not to Buy: Why We Overshop, and How to Stop*. (South Africa: Trumpeter, 2008).
- T.D. Schulman, *Bought Out and Spent! Recovery from Compulsive Shopping and Spending*. (West Conshohocken, PA: Infinity Publishing, 2008).

Twelve Step Groups

- Debtors Anonymous, 800-421-2383, www.debtorsanonymous.org
- Spenders Anonymous, www.spenders.org

Online Video Gaming Addiction Resources

General Information

- Useful information on video game addiction can be found at www.video-game-addiction.org.
- A medical perspective on video game addiction can be found at www.webmd.com/mental-health/features/video-game-addiction-no-fun.

Books

- A.P. Doan, B. Strickland, and D. Gentile, *Hooked on Games: The Lure and Cost of Video Game and Internet Addiction*. (Singapore: FEP International, 2012).
- K. Roberts, *Cyber Junkie: Escape the Gaming and Internet Trap*. (Center City, MN: Hazelden, 2010).

Twelve Step Groups

- On-Line Gamers Anonymous (OLGA), www.olganon.org.
- Recoveries Anonymous (RA), www.r-a.org/i-video-game-addiction.htm.

< 174 >

Sex, Porn, and Love Addiction Resources

General Information

- The Sexual Recovery Institute provides a significant amount of useful information at www.sexualrecovery.com.
- The Society for the Advancement of Sexual Health provides a significant amount of useful information at www.sash.net. This includes contact information for Twelve Step programs and for knowledgeable therapists by state and city.
- The International Institute for Trauma & Addiction Professionals provides a significant amount of useful information at www.iitap.com.

Books

- R. Weiss and J. Schneider, *Always Turned On: Facing Sex Addiction in the Digital Age.* (Carefree, AZ: Gentle Path Press, 2014).
- R. Weiss, *Cruise Control: Understanding Sex Addiction in Gay Men* (Second Edition). (Carefree, AZ: Gentle Path Press, 2013).
- G. Collins and A. Adleman, *Breaking the Cycle: Free Yourself from Sex Addiction, Porn Obsession, and Shame.* (Oakland, CA: New Harbinger Publications, 2011).
- P. Carnes, *Out of the Shadows: Understanding Sex Addiction.* (Center City, MN: Hazelden, 2001).
- P. Carnes, *Contrary to Love: Helping the Sexual Addict.* (Center City, MN: Hazelden, 1989).
- P. Carnes, *Don't Call it Love: Recovery from Sex Addiction.* (NY: Bantam, 1992).
- D. Corley and J.P. Schneider, *Disclosing Secrets: An Addict's Guide to What, to Whom and How Much to Reveal.* (N. Charleston, SC: CreateSpace, 2012).
- K. McDaniel, *Ready to Heal: Breaking Free of Addictive Relationships.* (Carefree, AZ: Gentle Path Press, 2012).
- M. Ferree, *No Stones: Women Redeemed from Sexual Addiction.* (Downers Grove, IL: IVP Books, 2010).
- The Augustine Fellowship, *Sex and Love Addicts Anonymous,*

< 175 >

The Basic Text for The Augustine Fellowship (San Antonio, TX: Augustine Fellowship, 1986).

Twelve Step Groups

- Sex Addicts Anonymous, 713-869-4902, www.saa-recovery.org
- Sex and Love Addicts Anonymous, 210-828-7900, www.slaafws.org
- Sexaholics Anonymous, 866-424-8777, www.sa.org
- Sexual Compulsives Anonymous, 310-859-5585, www.sca-recovery.org

Substance Abuse Resources

General Information

- General information can be found on the Substance Abuse and Mental Health Services Administration's website, www.samhsa.gov.
- General information can be found through National Council on Alcoholism and Drug Dependence, www.ncadd.org.
- General information can be found on the National Institute on Drug Abuse website, www.drugabuse.gov.
- Treatment-specific information can be found at www.promises.com.
- Treatment-specific information can be found at www.recoveryranch.com.

Books

- P. Carnes, S. Carnes, and J. Bailey, *Facing Addiction: Starting Recovery from Alcohol and Drugs.* (Carefree, AZ: Gentle Path Press, 2011).
- Anonymous, *Alcoholics Anonymous.* (New York: AA World Services).
- Anonymous, *Twelve Steps and Twelve Traditions.* (New York: AA World Services, 2002).
- Anonymous, *Living Sober.* (New York: AA World Services, 2002).

< 176 >

- World Services Office, *Narcotics Anonymous*. (New York: AA World Services, 2008).
- Anonymous, *Twenty Four Hours a Day*. (Center City, MN: Hazelden, 2013).
- S. Marshall, *Pocket Sponsor, 24/7 Back to the Basics Support for Addiction Recovery*. (Kingman, AZ: Day by Day, Recovery Resources, 2007).
- J. Ortberg, *The Me I Want to Be: Becoming God's Best Version of You*. (Grand Rapids, MI: Zondervan, 2009).

Twelve Step Groups
- Alcoholics Anonymous, 212-870-3400, www.aa.org
- Cocaine Anonymous, 800-347-8998, www.ca.org
- Crystal Meth Anonymous, 855-638-4383, www.crystalmeth.org
- Heroin Anonymous, www.heroin-anonymous.org
- Marijuana Anonymous, 800-766-6779, www.marijuana-anonymous.org
- Narcotics Anonymous, 818-773-9999, www.na.org
- Nicotine Anonymous, www.nicotine-anonymous.org
- Pills Anonymous, www.pillsanonymous.org

Resources for Partners and Families

General Information
- Useful information for partners of addicts can be found at www.addictiontreatmentmagazine.com/addiction/drug-addiction/how-to-deal-with-your-partners-drug-abuse, and at ezinearticles.com/?Partners-of-Addicts---5-Steps-to-Coping-With-Life-As-the-Partner-of-an-Addict&id=2125557.
- Useful information on codependency can be found at www.nmha.org/go/codependency.

Books
- M. Beattie, *Codependents Guide to the Twelve Steps*. (New York: Touchstone, 1992).

< 177 >

- S. Carnes, *Mending a Shattered Heart: A Guide to Partners of Sex Addicts*. (Carefree, AZ: Gentle Path Press, 2011).
- P. Collins and G. Collins, *A Couple's Guide to Sexual Addiction: A Step-by-Step Plan to Rebuild Trust and Restore Intimacy*. (NY: Harper & Row, 2011).
- J. Schneider and B. Schneider, *Sex, Lies, and Forgiveness* (Third Edition). (Tucson, AZ: Recovery Resources Press, 2004).
- P. Carnes, D. Laaser and M. Laaser, *Open Hearts: Renewing Relationships with Recovery, Romance & Reality*. (Carefree, AZ: Gentle Path Press, 1999).
- P. Mellody, A.W. Miller and J.K. Miller, *Facing Codependence: What It Is, Where It Comes From, How It Sabotages Our Lives*. (New York: Harper & Row, 1989).
- M. Beattie, *Codependent No More: How to Stop Controlling Others and Start Caring for Yourself*. (Center City, MN: Hazelden, 1986).
- M. Beattie, *Codependent No More Workbook*. (Center City, MN: Hazelden, 2011).
- J.P. Schneider and D. Corley, *Surviving Disclosure: A Partner's Guide for Healing the Betrayal of Intimate Trust*. (N. Charleston, SC: CreateSpace, 2012).
- M. Corcoran, *A House Interrupted: A Wife's Story of Recovering from Her Husband's Sex Addiction* (Carefree, AZ: Gentle Path Press, 2011).

Twelve Step Groups
- Adult Children of Alcoholics, 310-534-1815, www.adultchildren.org
- Al-Anon, 800-344-2666, www.al-anon-alateen.org
- Alateen (ages 12 to 17), 800-356-9996, www.al-anon-alateen.org
- Co-Anon, www.co-anon.org
- Co-Dependents Anonymous, 602-277-7991, www.codependents.org
- Co-Dependents of Sex Addicts (COSA), 612-537-6904, www.cosa-recovery.org

< 178 >

- Families Anonymous, 310-815-8010, www.familiesanonymous.org
- Recovering Couples Anonymous, 314-997-9808, www.recovering-couples.org
- S-Anon, 615-833-3152, www.sanon.org

Other Twelve Step Recovery Groups

- Clutterers Anonymous, https://sites.google.com/site/clutterersanonymous/Home?pli=1
- Emotions Anonymous, 651-647-9712, www.emotionsanonymous.org
- Emotional Health Anonymous, emotionalhealthanonymous.org
- Food Addicts in Recovery Anonymous, www.foodaddicts.org
- Food Addicts Anonymous, www.foodaddictsanonymous.org
- Overeaters Anonymous, www.oa.org
- Survivors of Incest Anonymous, 410-282-3400, www.siawso.org
- Underearners Anonymous, http://underearnersanonymous.org
- Workaholics Anonymous, www.workaholics-anonymous.org

Other General Resources

- International Institute for Trauma and Addiction Professionals (IITAP), 480-575-6853, www.iitap.com
- National Council on Alcoholism and Drug Dependence, www.ncadd.org
- National Institute on Drug Abuse website, www.drugabuse.gov
- Runaway and Suicide Hotline, 800-Run-Away, www.1800runaway.org

< 179 >

- Sexual Addiction Resources, Dr. Patrick Carnes, www.sexhelp. com
- Society for the Advancement of Sexual Health, 770-541-9912, www.sash.net
- Substance Abuse and Mental Health Services Administration's website, www.samhsa.gov

< 180 >

GLOSSARY

Getting Up to Speed with Tech Terms

adult friend-finder apps. These apps are most often "friend finders" in name only. They are really sex-locator apps, designed for casual hook-ups. Users can find currently available, geographically desirable sex partners in much the same way that other apps can locate a nearby sushi bar. Log on and instantly see a grid of users' pictures, sorted by gender and arranged from nearest to farthest away. Simply tap on a picture and a brief profile of that user appears, along with the option to chat, send pictures (sext), or share your own location. If the interest is mutual, the two users make a plan to meet. Whatever happens next is up to them.

apps. Apps are software that can be downloaded to smartphones or tablets to perform a specific function. Many people download "navigation" apps that allow them to type in an address and then get driving directions. Other apps can help you find a restaurant, play games, or listen to music.

Ashley Madison. This is an adult friend-finder (sex locator) website and app for married people looking to cheat on their spouse. The company slogan is "Life is short, have an affair." With sixteen million members, it is among the world's most financially viable social media websites/apps.

avatar. This is a visual representation of a real-world person. People use these as part of their online persona. Avatars are usually animated figures. Most often it is an idealized version of some part of the user.

< 181 >

Bang with Friends. Popular with young adults, this adult friend-finder (sex locator) app helps people determine which of their existing Facebook friends might be interested in "benefits" (no-strings-attached sex).

BBS. See *bulletin board system*.

Blendr. Blendr is an adult friend-finder (sex locator) app used by straight people for casual hookups.

blog. This is a hybrid word, a combination of *web* and *log*. Typically, blogs (written by bloggers) are either online journals or ongoing discussions on a particular topic. Blogs consist of discrete entries known as "posts." Sometimes blogs are informative. Most blogs are personal in nature. Often, "personal" blogs stick to a single basic topic—travel, getting married, pregnancy, the local baseball team, and so on. The difference between blogs and static websites is that blogs are interactive. Followers can leave comments and sometimes even send messages directly to other readers. Often, the blogger will respond directly to comments about the blog post, even writing new material based on that feedback. In this way, blogging is a form of social networking.

bulletin board system (BBS). This is essentially an online bulletin board that allows users to upload and download information, messages, and files. BBS was the predecessor of chat rooms and the modern Internet and is rarely used today.

chat rooms. Chat rooms are a direct offshoot of email. They provide users with a way to communicate in real time by sending messages (instant "group emails") to people who are "visiting" the same chat room. Most chat rooms are aimed at a specific group of people, providing a forum for those individuals to meet and share information about their common interests and to participate in open or sometimes moderated discussions on that particular topic. In this way, chat rooms create a virtual educational or social community in an otherwise divergent and disconnected world.

< 182 >

Chatroulette. This video and audio (or text) chat site randomly pairs strangers from around the world for web-based interactions. Patrons turn on their webcam, hit start, and then are paired with a chat partner chosen at random. Spin the wheel and see who you get! At any point users may leave the current chat by hitting the "next" button, and the program initiates another arbitrary connection. This is very popular with online exhibitionists.

co-occuring disorder. This refers to someone having one or more addictions combined with one or more psychiatric disorders. Dual diagnosis is an older term for co-occurring disorders.

cyberbullying. This refers to the deliberate, repeated, and hostile use of the Internet and related technologies to harm other people.

cyberstalking. This is the use of the Internet or other electronic means to stalk or harass someone.

digital gaming addiction. Extreme use of computer and video games—use to the point that it interferes with daily life—is considered a digital gaming addiction.

email. Also known as "electronic mail," this is the nearly instantaneous transmission of written communication. It's like sending a letter via the U.S. Postal Service, but faster and cheaper. Over the years, email technology has evolved to allow multiple people to be contacted simultaneously (via email subscriber lists). Furthermore, large files—including pictures, music, and videos—can now be transmitted easily and relatively quickly (as attachments).

emoticon. A composite of the words *emotion* and *icon*, an emoticon is a visual representation of a facial expression. These textual symbols are used to express a person's mood or feelings, helping to clarify the writer's intent. A common emoticon is built using a colon, a dash, and close-parentheses to create a "smile."

< 183 >

Facebook. Launched in February 2004, this website has over one billion members. Users sign up, create a personal profile that often includes *a lot* of personal information. Typically, Facebook profiles contain photos, lists of personal interests, contact information, and various other personal data. Once enrolled, users "friend" other users (which means they're asking them to "follow" their posts and vice versa); exchange messages; post pictures, videos, and hyperlinks; "like" the posts of other people; and generally keep track of one another's comings and goings. To address privacy concerns, Facebook now allows users to select from a variety of privacy settings, limiting who can see parts of their profile—though a member's name and profile picture are accessible to all Facebook users unless that member specifically blocks someone.

FaceTime. A video telephone/voice chat service similar to Skype where you can conduct one-to-one video calls between Apple users. This is a free service that requires an Apple ID and Wi-Fi connection.

Foursquare. This smartphone app allows registered users to post their location. Users are often hyper-specific, "Eating tacos at Joe's on 26th and Main." Foursquare "check-ins" can be automatically posted to Facebook and Twitter.

Grindr. This is an adult friend-finder (sex locator) app for gay men.

hookup apps. See *adult friend-finder apps*.

hosted porn galleries. These are free porn galleries similar to "thumbnail" sites. Unlike the thumbnail sites, however, hosted sites provide full-size images and full-length amateur videos, with links to the commercial site(s) in case the viewer wants to see (and is willing to pay for) a larger selection of similar material.

hyperlink. This can be included in an email, blog, or any other digital posting. When users click on the hyperlink, they are automatically redirected to a specific webpage. If you want all of your friends to read a

< 184 >

certain article, you send them an email with a hyperlink, making it very easy for them to access what you want them to see.

infidelity. In the digital age, infidelity is best defined as the breaking of trust in an intimate relationship caused by the keeping of secrets.

Instagram. This photo-sharing and social networking service lets users take pictures and share them, either manually or automatically, on social media sites like Facebook and Twitter. The photos are distinctly square, like old Polaroid images, as opposed to the usual four-to-three ratio of digital photos.

instant messaging (IM). This allows people who meet in a chat room to take their conversation into a more private setting. Basically, instant messaging is a "closed" chat room in which people can IM.

IRL. Text-speak for "in real life."

MABs (multi-author blogs). Most often, blogs are written by a single individual. However, multi-author blogs are becoming more common. These are often the collective work of universities, think tanks, activists, political groups, professional groups, or institutions.

micro-blogging. See *Twitter*.

moderated dating sites. Some dating sites are carefully moderated, meaning they use an algorithm of some sort to provide potential "matches," whereas others are non-moderated free-for-alls where members peruse profiles and digitally contact whomever they want. The two most popular dating sites are Match.com and eHarmony.com, which are both moderated. Match.com bases its matchmaking on the Myers-Briggs Personality Test, while eHarmony.com uses "secret key dimensions of compatibility," whatever that means.

< 185 >

MySpace. Initially, MySpace was the most popular social networking site. It has long been surpassed by Facebook, Twitter, and several others. Today it has a strong emphasis on popular music.

newsgroups. These are basically an advanced electronic bulletin board system. Much of the content posted is pornographic. Newsgroups are not as popular as they once were since there are now so many mainstream porn sites (both free and for pay). However, they are still used as a way to post illegal imagery (child porn, bestiality, and so on).

online porn sites. Most online pornography is accessed via porn websites. In the beginning, porn sites were nearly always commercial sites to which men (and sometimes women) subscribed so they could view and download stories, still images, and videos for a daily, monthly, or annual fee. Commercial porn sites in foreign countries (particularly Russian sites) are known to overcharge or otherwise abuse users' credit card information. Porn sites and porn links are also notorious for spreading viruses and for "redirecting" users to things they don't want to see. Today, much online porn is free and made by amateurs.

online profiles. People joining a new social media, dating, or other website sign up as members and then create a profile, providing varying amounts of personal information. Almost all social media and dating sites allow members to upload photos and videos and to browse the photos and videos of others. Most sites also offer services like instant messaging, voice, and video chat.

peer-to-peer file sharing. Friends and online acquaintances sometimes use this as a way to send files back and forth. Often, these files are pornographic in nature. It is used less frequently now than in years past, though it is still the most common way to privately exchange illegal imagery (child porn, bestiality, and so on).

PinkCupid. This is an adult friend-finder (primarily a sex locator) app for lesbians.

< 186 >

profiles. See *online profiles*.

PTP. See *peer-to-peer file sharing*.

sexnology. It refers to technologies, usually digital technologies, specifically designed to generate or enhance sexual pleasure.

sexting. This is a hybrid word that combines *sex* and *texting*. It means exactly what you might expect—the sending of sexually explicit messages and/or photographs. This is sometimes done using an IM program on a computer but more often via the texting capability of mobile phones. Sexting ranges, essentially, from on-the-go digital flirting to virtual exhibitionism.

Skout. This is an adult friend-finder (primarily a sex locator) app for straight people.

Skype. This very popular video chat service allows users to communicate using a webcam and a microphone, or a webcam and IMs. Calls can be placed on traditional telephone networks (both land lines and cellular). The service also allows file transfer and video conferencing.

social discovery apps. These apps are designed to alert you to the nearby presence of people you don't know but might like to know. Basically, they are digital yentas—meddling busybodies intent on hooking you up, through your smartphone, with people they think you should know. They work by applying algorithms to the personal data you and others provide on social media networks like Facebook and LinkedIn. The apps theoretically direct you toward nearby people who share your interests, work in the same field, or know some of the same people you know, thereby increasing your odds of creating new friendships, business partnerships, sexual liaisons, and even long-term relationships.

social media. Social media blends technology and social interaction, thereby producing interactive online content that is both generated and

< 187 >

consumed by the same population. We create it, we share it, and we read and/or look at it. The professional/industrial media sometimes refers to social media as CGM, or consumer-generated media. Social media allows us to meet, interact, and develop intimate personal and sometimes even sexual relationships with virtually anyone else, anywhere, anytime. The most prominent social media sites in the United States are Facebook and Twitter.

text-speak. Because people can only type so fast, a form of online shorthand has evolved and become part of our regular lexicon. Abbreviations such as LOL (laugh out loud), ROTFL (rolling on the floor laughing), BFF (best friend forever), BRB (be right back), and TTYL (talk to you later) have actually achieved dictionary status. Symbols and shortened versions of words are also common, like "Mt u @ chnse rstrnt @ 7." This evolved (or maybe devolved) version of our language is a direct outcome of digital interconnectivity.

thumbnail porn galleries. These are websites that post links to commercial porn sites, providing a free sample of what's available in the form of thumbnail images or partial-length videos, which usually end before the "money shot" with a message like, "To see the full-length video visit www.paywebsite.com."

Tinder. Popular among young adults, Tinder is an adult friend-finder (primarily a sex locator) app for heterosexuals. It uses Facebook profiles to create potential matches.

Twitter. The newest and currently the most popular form of blogging is "micro-blogging." On Twitter, users write messages (micro-blogs) up to 140 characters long—about the length of a normal sentence—posting them via computers, smartphones, and other mobile devices. These messages are known as "tweets" and are read by "followers." There are well over 100 million active Twitter users who collectively tweet more than 175 million times per day.

< 188 >

webcam. A webcam is a video camera that feeds its imagery in real time to a computer, digital device, or computer network. These images can then be interactively viewed by whomever is at the receiving end of the exchange.

webcam porn. This type of porn can be used by a group of members of an adult pay site or can be purchased on a pay-per-view basis by one person. In this private scenario, the person paying directs the person or persons "acting" to engage in various sexual acts. Companies around the world set up websites for performers and manage the finances. Essentially these companies are online strip clubs, gathering up the dollar bills and distributing a percentage of the money to the performers.

Wikipedia. This online encyclopedia has over 25 million articles in 285 languages and is written and edited by volunteers. It is the largest and most popular reference work of all time.

video chat. Facilitated via webcam, this lets people see one another while they engage in traditional text-based chat or, if the chat service has an audio feature (as many now do) interact in real time with both video and voice—sort of like the science fiction video phone of yesteryear.

YouTube. This video-sharing website allows users to post and view homemade or commercial videos. YouTube videos are often hyper-linked to and from social networking sites.

< 189 >

NOTES

Introduction: The Historical Impact of Technology on Human Relationships and Communication

1. Oliver Sacks, *Musicophilia: Tales of Music and the Brain* (New York: Knopf, 2007).
2. Alvin Toffler, *Future Shock* (New York: Bantam Books, 1970), 3.
3. Ibid. 13–14.
4. Lewis H. Morgan, *Ancient Society, or, Researches in the Lines of Human Progress from Savagery through Barbarism to Civilization* (London: MacMillan & Co Reprinted Courtesy Cornell University, 1877).
5. Gerhard E. Lenski, *Power and Privilege: A Theory of Social Stratification* (New York: McGraw Hill, 1966).
6. Toffler, *Future Shock*, 15–16.
7. "The Internet Big Picture: World Internet Users and Population Stats," Internet World Stats, accessed December 31, 2011, http://www.internetworldstats.com/stats.htm.

Chapter One: The New Generation Gap

1. Marc Prensky, "Digital Natives, Digital Immigrants", *On the Horizon*, September/October 2001, http://www.marcprensky.com/writing/Prensky%20-%20Digital%20Natives,%20Digital%20Immigrants%20-%20Part1.pdf (and November/December 2001,. http://www.scribd.com/doc/9800/Prensky-Digital-Natives-Digital-Immigrants-Part2).
2. H. Schuman and J. Scott, "Generations and Collective Memories," *American Sociological Review* 54, no. 3 (1989), 359–81.
3. Kathleen Shaputis, *The Crowded Nest Syndrome: Surviving the Return*

< 191 >

of Adult Children (Olympia, WA: Clutter Fairy Publishing, 2004).

4. Katie Zezema, "The Case for Cursive," *New York Times*, April 27, 2011, http://www.nytimes.com/2011/04/28/us/28/cursive/html.

5. Christina Hoag, "Some States Opt to Keep Cursive in Curriculum," *Arizona Daily Star*, November 25, 2012, A15.

6. Philip Hensher, "The Lost Art of the Handwritten Note," *Wall Street Journal*, December 28, 2012.

7. Sheng Hui, "Calligraphy in the Age of Texting," Yanzhao Evening News, quoted in *The Week*, December 28, 2012, 15.

8. Mary Quigley, "Digital Generation Gap," *Huffington Post*, July 2, 2012, http://www.huffingtonpost.com/mary-quigley/digital-natives-classroom_b_1643372.html.

9. Ibid.

10. Tamar Lewin, "Universities Reshaping Education on the Web," *New York Times*, July 17, 2012, A12.

11. "Learning New Lessons," *The Economist*, December 22, 2012, 101.

12. Quigley, "Digital Generation Gap."

13. David Koeppel, "Baby Boomers Are Putting the Smackdown on Gen Y at Work," The Fiscal Times, November 12, 2011, http://www.businessinsider.com/babyboomers-are-putting-the-smackdown-on-gen-y-at-work-2011-11.

14. Ibid.

15. Stephanie Hoffman, "Gen-Y Would Break Rules for BYOD," *Fortinet (Fortiblog)*, June 19, 2012, http://blog.fortinet.com/study-gen-y-would-break-rules-for-byod/.

16. "Boomers vs. Generation Y: Bridging The Generation Gap at the Office," *Huffington Post*, August 22, 2012, http://www.huffingtonpost.com/2011/11/18/bridging-the-generation-gap_n_1102396.html.

17. "The Net Generation Unplugged," *The Economist*, May 4, 2010, http://www.economist.com/node/15582279.

18. Morley Winograd and Michael D. Hais, "Bridging Today's Generation Gap," *National Journal*, June 15, 2012, http://www.nationaljournal.com/thenextamerica/demographics/bridging-

< 192 >

today-s-generation-gap-20120615.

19. G. S. O'Keefe, K. C. Clarke-Pearson, and Council on Communication and Media, "Clinical Report—The Impact of Social Media on Children, Adolescents, and Families," *Pediatrics* 127 (2011): 800–804.

20. "Social Isolation and New Technology: How the Internet and Mobile Phones Impact Americans' Social Networks," Pew Internet & American Life Project, accessed August 22, 2012, http://www.pewinternet.org/Static-Pages/Trend-Data-(Teens)/Teen-Gadget-Ownership.aspx.

21. "Teens, Smartphones, and Texting," Pew Internet & American Life Project, March 19, 2012, http://www.pewinternet.org/Reports/2012/Teens-and-smartphones/Summary-of-findings.aspx.

22. Martha Irvine, "Is Texting Ruining the Art of Conversation?" Associated Press, accessed from *Huffington Post*, June 3, 2012, http://www.huffingtonpost.com/2012/06/03/text-messaging-texting-conversation_n_1566408.html.

23. Ibid.

24. Timothy VanSlyke, "Digital Natives, Digital Immigrants," *Commentary*, May/June 2003, http://depd.wisc.edu/html/TSarticles/Digital%20Natives.htm.

Chapter Two: The Internet: Where Everyone Can Be Heard

1. P. M. Valkenburg and J. Peter, "Online Communication among Adolescents: An Integrated Model of Its Attraction, Opportunities, and Risks," *Journal of Adolescent Health* 48 (2011): 121–27.

2. A. L. Ball, "The Spotlight Dims and Shyness Sets In," *New York Times*, July 8, 2012.

3. "Wikipedia," Wikipedia, accessed February 12, 2013, http://en.wikipedia.org/wiki/Wikipedia.

4. Jim Giles, "Special Report: Internet, Encyclopedias Go Head to Head," *Nature*, December 15, 2005, 900–901.

5. Jeff Howe, "The Rise of Crowdsourcing," *Wired*, June 2006,

< 193 >

http://www.wired.com/wired/archive/14.06/crowds.html.

6. Nate Lanxon, "How the Oxford English Dictionary Started Out Like Wikipedia," *Wired*, January 13, 2011, http://www.wired. co.uk/news/archive/2011-01/13/the-oxford-english-wiktionary.

7. "The Science behind FoldIt," FoldIt, accessed November 2, 2012, http://fold.it/portal/info/science.

8. Jane McGonigal, *Reality Is Broken: Why Games Make Us Better and How They Can Change the World* (New York: Penguin, 2011), 219–32.

9. A. Park, "Social Media Are Changing How We Diagnose Disease," *Time Magazine*, August 6, 2012.

10. J. P. Schneider, W. B. Hinshaw, C. Su, and P Solow, "Atypical Femur Fractures: 81 Individual Personal Histories," *Journal of Clinical Endocrinology and Metabolism* 97 (2012): 4324–28.

11. "The Roar of the Crowd: Crowdsourcing Is Transforming the Science of Psychology," *Economist*, May 26, 2012, 77–78.

12. B. Ghosh and D. Dias, "Change Agent," *Time Magazine*, April 9, 2012, 39–43.

13. Y. Marzouki, I. Skandrani-Marzouki, M. Bejaoui, H. Hammoudi, and T. Bellaj, "The Contribution of Facebook to the 2011 Tunisian Revolution: A Cyberpsychological Insight," *Cyberpsychology, Behavior and Social Networking* 15, no. 5 (2012) : 237–44.

14. "Malala in 2011: My People Need Me," CNN, accessed February 12, 2013, http://www.cnn.com/video/#/video/world/2012/10/10/sayah-2011-interview-malala-yousufzai.cnn.

15. Fareed Zakaria, "Technology Boosting China People Power," Tibet Sun and CNN, August 4, 2012, http://www.tibetsun.com/tech_news/2012/08/04/technology-boosting-china-people-power.

16. Ibid.

17. Ibid.

18. Pamela Paul, "Kramer.com vs. Kramer.com," *New York Times*, November 25, 2012, Styles, 1.

19. Boots on Ground, *Ways to Communicate with a Soldier in Iraq*, accessed November 1, 2012, http://www.bootsonground.com/iraq-communications.htm.

< 194 >

20. Daniel Jones, "College Romance," *New York Times*, May 1, 2011, Sunday Styles, 5.
21. Ibid.

Chapter Three: Parenting Healthy Children in the Digital Age

1. Nicole Laporte, "Where Apps Become Child's Play," *New York Times*, July 8, 2012, 3.
2. Ibid.
3. Ibid.
4. Lisa Eliot, "The Truth about Boys and Girls," *Scientific American*, May/June 2010, 22.
5. Ibid.
6. Karen Schrock, "Once Learned, Never Forgotten," *Scientific American*, May/June 2010, 7.
7. American Academy of Pediatrics. *Children, Adolescents, and the Media*. October 28, 2013.
8. Laporte, "Where Apps Become Child's Play."
9. Sherry Turkle, *Alone Together: Why We Expect More from Technology and Less from Each Other* (New York: Basic Books, 2011), 56.
10. Hanna Rosin, "The Touch-Screen Generation," *Atlantic*, April 2013, http://www.theatlantic.com/magazine/archive/2013/04/the-touch-screen-generation/309250/.
11. Ibid.
12. Ibid.
13. Ibid.
14. Lisa Guernsey, *Screen Time: How Electronic Media—From Baby Videos to Educational Software—Affects Your Child* (Basic Books: Philadelphia, 2007).
15. B. J. Casey and R. M. Jones, "Neurobiology of the Adolescent Brain and Behavior: Implications for Substance Use Disorders," *Journal of the American Academy of Child and Adolescent Psychiatry* 49 (2010): 1189–1201.
16. B. J. Casey, R. M. Jones, and L. H. Somerville, "Braking and Accelerating the Adolescent Brain," *Journal of Research on Adolescence* 21 (2011): 21–33.

< 195 >

17. NPD Group, *Extreme Gamers Spend Two Full Days Per Week Playing Video Games*, May 27, 2010, https://www.npd.com/wps/portal/npd/us/news/press-releases/pr_100527b/.

18. Jane McGonigal, *Reality Is Broken: Why Games Make Us Better and How They Change the World* (New York: Penguin Press, 2011), citing Entertainment Software Association, Essential Facts about the Game Industry: 2010 Sales, Demographic and Usage Data, www.theesa.com/facts/pdfs/ESA_Essential_Facts_2010.PDF (Jun 16, 2010).

19. NPD Group, *Extreme Gamers Spend Two Full Days Per Week Playing Video Games*.

20. Don Tapscott, *How Digital Technology Has Changed the Brain*, Business Week, November 10, 2008, http://www.businessweek.com/stories/2008-11-10/how-digital-technology-has-changed-the-brainbusinessweek-business-news-stock-market-and-financial-advice.

21. Ibid.

22. J. Wolak, D. Finkelhor, and K.J . Mitchell, "How Often Are Teens Arrested for Sexting? Data From a National Sample of Police Cases," *Pediatrics* 129 (2012): 1–12.

23. C. Sabina, J. Wolak, and D. Finkelhor, "The Nature and Dynamics of Internet Pornography Exposure for Youth," *Cyperpsychology & Behavior* 11, no. 6 (2008): 691–93.

24. *The Stats on Internet Pornography*, accessed February 14, 2013, http://thedinfographics.com/2011/12/23/internet-pornography-statistics/.

Chapter Four: Sex, Tech, and Love

1. A. Cooper, D. A. Putnam, L. A. Planchon, and S. C. Boies, "Online Sexual Compulsivity: Getting Tangled in the Net," *Sexual Addiction & Compulsivity* 6, no. 2 (1999): 79–104.

2. Jesse Fox and Katie M. Warber, "Romantic Relationship Development in the Age of Facebook: An Exploratory Study of Emerging Adults' Perceptions, Motives, and Behaviors," *Cyberpsychology, Behavior, and Social Networking* 16, no. 1 (2013): 3–7.

< 196 >

3. Ki Mae Hussner, "Facebook as Foreplay? Survey Says Social Media Leads to Sex Faster," ABC News, January 26, 2011, http://abcnews.go.com/Technology/facebook-foreplay-survey-social-media-leads-sex-faster/story?id=12767315#.UFj0iY1mRng.

4. "Michigan Study Says "Sexting" Is the Modern-Day Way of Flirting," ClickOn Detroit, July 25, 2012, http://www.clickondetroit.com/news/news/Michigan-study-says-sexting-is-the-modern-day-way-of-flirting/-/4714498/15697310/-/8i9r2tz/-/ind.

5. Hussner, "Facebook as Foreplay?"

6. Ibid.

7. The Married Chick blog, "'I Love You in the Digital Age," MSN, August 1, 2012, http://living.msn.com/love-relationships/the-married-chick-blog-post?post=dd46c0fd-4be1-4853-a181-c831abec5f69&_blg=3.

8. Michael Stewart (book), Charles Strouse (music), Lee Adams (lyrics), *Bye Bye Birdie* (Broadway Musical), Martin Beck Theatre, 54th Street Theatre, Shubert Theater (April 1960–October 1961).

9. "Facebook User Statistics 2012," AnsonAlex.com, February 20, 2012, http://ansonalex.com/infographics/facebook-user-statistics-2012-infographic/.

10. TED Talks (Technology, Entertainment, and Design Talks) are a global set of conferences owned by the Sapling Foundation, formed in 1984 to disseminate "ideas worth sharing." The best TED Talks are videotaped and posted online for free viewing.

11. Philip G. Zimbardo and Nikita Duncan, *The Demise of Guys: Why Boys Are Struggling and What We Can Do About It* (Amazon Digital Services, 2012).

12. Ibid.

13. Roger Pulvers, "Reversing Japan's Rising Sex Aversion May Depend on a Rebirth of Hope," *Japan Times*, April 29, 2012, http://www.japantimes.co.jp/text/fl20120429rp.html.

14. Ibid.

15. Zimbardo and Duncan, *Demise of Guys*. TED Talks.

16. Charlotte Kasl, *Women, Sex, and Addiction: A Search for Love and*

< 197 >

Power (New York: Ticknor & Fields, 1989).

17. "The Stats on Internet Pornography," Infographics, accessed September 27, 2012, http://thedinfographics.com/2011/12/23/internet-pornography-statistics/.

18. M. C. Ferree, "Women and the Web: Cybersex Activity and Implications," *Sexual and Relationship Therapy* 18, no. 3 (2003): 385–93.

19. Ibid.

20. Stephanie Pappas, "Porn and Relationships: Men's Pornography Use Tied to Lower Self-Esteem in Female Partners," *Huffington Post* (citing research by Destin Stewart), June 1, 2012, http://www.huffingtonpost.com/2012/06/01/porn-relationships-men-female-partner-self-esteem_n_1562821.html?ref=women.

21. Ian Kerner, *Do Women Like Porn as Much as Men?* CNN Health, April 28, 2011, http://thechart.blogs.cnn.com/2011/04/28/do-women-like-porn-as-much-as-men/.

22. Ibid.

23. Norman Doidge, *The Brain That Changes Itself: Stories of Personal Triumph from the Frontiers of Brain Science* (London: Penguin, 2007).

24. Jeremy Hsu, "Digital Age Sex: What a Robot Has That You Don't," June 9, 2011, http://www.msnbc.msn.com/id/43342345/ns/technology_and_science-innovation/t/digital-age-sex-what-robot-has-you-dont.

25. Ibid.

26. David Levy, *Love and Sex with Robots: The Evolution of Human-Robot Relationships* (New York: HarperCollins, 2007), 22.

27. Rachel Dretzin, *Digital Nation: Life on the Virtual Frontier*, PBS Films (Frontline) 2010.

28. Levy, *Love and Sex with Robots*, 9.

29. The Decline of Marriage and Rise of New Families," Pew Research Center, December 19, 2010, "http://pewresearch.org/pubs/1802/decline-marriage-rise-new-families.

30. Stephanie Coontz, *Marriage, a History: How Love Conquered Marriage* (London: Penguin Books, 2005), 15.

31. Kate Bolick, "All the Single Ladies," *Atlantic*, November 2011,

< 198 >

http://www.theatlantic.com/magazine/archive/2011/11/all-the-single-ladies/308654/.

32. Hanna Rosin, "Boys on the Side," *Atlantic*, September 2012, http://www.theatlantic.com/magazine/archive/2012/09/boys-on-the-side/309062/?single_page=true.

Chapter Five: Online Vulnerability: The Dark Side of the Force

1. S. Marche, "Is Facebook Making Us Lonely?" *Atlantic Monthly*, May 2, 2012, http://www.theatlantic.com/magazine/archive/2012/05/is-facebook-making-us-lonely/8930.

2. Marche, "Is Facebook Making Us Lonely?"

3. AARP, *Loneliness among Older Adults: A National Survey of Adults 45+*, September 2012, http://www.aarp.org/personal-growth/transitions/info-09-2010/loneliness_2010.html.

4. Ibid.

5. Tracii Ryan and Sophia Xenos, "Who Uses Facebook? An Investigation into the Relationship between the Big Five, Shyness, Narcissism, Loneliness, and Facebook Usage," *Computers in Human Behavior* 27, no. 5 (2011): 1658–64.

6. Marche, "Is Facebook Making Us Lonely?"

7. Ryan and Xenos, "Who Uses Facebook?" 1658–64.

8. "The Way We Were in 2012," *The Week*, December 28, 2012, 20.

9. Catherine Saint Louis, "In the Facebook Era, Reminders of Loss after Families Fracture," *New York Times*, June 15, 2012, A1.

10. Ibid.

11. Meredith Fineman, "Breaking Up, Digital Style: Learning to Forget," *Huffington Post*, December 6, 2012, http://www.huffingtonpost.com/meredith-fineman/breaking-up-digital-style_b_2251232.html.

12. E. Toll, "A Piece of My Mind: The Cost of Technology," *Journal of the American Medical Association* 307, no. 23 (2012).

13. C. Marshall, "Few Tickets Issued Here Despite New Texting Law," *Arizona Daily Star*, June 25, 2012, A1.

14. Ki Mae Hussner, *Facebook as Foreplay? Survey Says Social Media Leads to Sex Faster*, ABC News, January 26, 2011, http://abcnews.

< 199 >

go.com/Technology/facebook-foreplay-survey-social-media-leads-sex-faster/story?id=12767315#.UFj0iY1mRng.

15. 2012 Cyberstalking Statistics, www.haltabuse.org/resources/stats/2012statistics.pdf

16. Sara Gates, "Adult Sexting on the Rise: 1 In 5 Americans Send Explicit Text Messages, Poll Finds," *Huffington Post*, June 8, 2012, http://www.huffingtonpost.com/2012/06/08/adult-sexting_n_1581234.html.

17. Ron Nixon, "Internet Use in Adoptions Cuts Two Ways, Report Says," *New York Times*, December 13, 2012.

18. M. T. Witty and T. Buchanan, "The Online Romance Scam: A Serious Cybercrime," *Cyberpsychology, Behavior, and Social Networking* 14, no. 3 (2012): 181–82.

19. James E Shiffer, "Online Scams Break Hearts, Bank Accounts," *Arizona Daily Star*, February 5, 2011.

20. Caitlin Dewey, "Even in Real Life, There Were Screens Between Us," *New York Times*, June 23, 2011.

21. J.P Schneider and B.H. Schneider, *Sex, Lies and Forgiveness: Couples Speak on Healing from Sex Addiction*, (Tucson, AZ: Recovery Resources Press, 2004)

Chapter Six: Technology and the"New" Addictions

1. American Society of Addiction Medicine, *Definition of Addiction*, accessed October 24, 2012, http://www.asam.org/research-treatment/definition-of-addiction.

2. Al Cooper, David Delmonico, and Ron Burg, "Cybersex Users, Abusers, and Compulsives: New Findings and Implications," in *Cybersex: The Dark Side of the Force* (A Special Issue of the *Journal Sexual Addiction & Compulsivity*), ed. Al Cooper (Oxford, UK: Taylor and Francis, 2000), 5–30.

3. Catherine Donaldson-Evans, *Junior Jackpot: Teen Gambling on the Rise*, May 17, 2006, http://www.foxnews.com/story/0,2933,195751,00.html.

4. Ibid.

5. Sheryl Sitman, "Teenagers and Compulsive Gambling Online,"

< 200 >

Ezine Articles, http://ezinearticles.com/?Teenagers-and-Compulsive-Gambling-Online&id=1320790.

6. W. B. Hagedorn and T. Young, "Identifying and Intervening with Students Exhibiting Signs of Gaming Addiction and other Addictive Behaviors: Implications for Professional School Counselors," *Professional School Counseling* 14, no. 4 (2011): 250–60.

7. "Hot Blooded Gaming," *Bad Parenting Leads to 15 Hour a Day Gaming Habit for Teen*, August 27, 2010, http://www.hotbloodedgaming.com/2010/08/27/bad-parenting-leads-to-15-hour-a-day-gaming-habit-for-teen/.

8. David Sack, *Why Fighting Addiction Can Feel Like a Game of Whac-a-mole*, http://blogs.psychcentral.com/addiction-recovery/2012/02/fighting-addiction-whac-a-mole/.

Chapter Seven: What's Coming Next Has Already Been

1. Abbey Stone, "Beyoncé Confirms Lip-Synching (Boo!) and Teases a Tour (Yay!) at NFL Press Conference," Hollywood.com, accessed February 20, 2013, http://www.hollywood.com/news/celebrities/49234496/beyonce-confirms-lip-syncing-boo-and-teases-a-tour-yay-at-nfl-press-conference?page=all.

2. Ted Anthony, "Can Reality Compete with Our Reality Show Expectations?" January 31, 2013, http://news.msn.com/pop-culture/can-reality-compete-with-our-reality-show-expectations.

3. Ibid.

4. "24 Hours: Unplugged," A Day without Media, accessed August 18, 2012, http://withoutmedia.wordpress.com.

5. Ibid.

6. Susan Greenfield, "Modern Technology Is Changing the Way Our Brains Work, Says Neuroscientist," *Daily Mail*, October 2, 2012, http://www.dailymail.co.uk/sciencetech/article-565207/Modern-technology-changing-way-brains-work-says-neuroscientist.html.

7. Ibid.

< 201 >

READING GROUP GUIDE

1. Regardless of when you were born, do you identify yourself as a digital immigrant or a digital native? What are you basing your response on?
2. What technological changes seen in your lifetime have specific meaning to you?
3. What are some of the advantages you have experienced because of these technological changes?
4. What are some of the disadvantages you have experienced because of these technological changes?
5. What would you say is the biggest difference between digital immigrants (born before 1980) and digital natives (born after 1980) and the way they communicate and interact with each other?
6. What can digital immigrants and digital natives learn from each other?
7. How are *today's kids* different than those children and teens of previous generations?
8. The American Academy of Pediatrics came out with some guidelines for parents on how to manage the role of digital technology. Do you think parents should set limitations on how much "screen time" children should have daily? Why?
9. In what ways have the Internet, cell phones, cable television, and other innovations changed the way in which you, your family, work colleagues and friends connect and communicate?
10. Do you know anyone who appears to be "addicted" to technology? What makes you think that?
11. In what ways have social media (Facebook, Twitter, Instagram, Snapchat, etc.) impacted your life?

< 203 >

12. How have work environments changed as a result of technology?

13. Have you ever had difficulty communicating at work with someone younger or older than you because you preferred different ways of communicating? For example, texting or emailing someone instead of setting up a face-to-face meeting?

14. What continued changes do you see evolving in your relationships and your work related to digital and social media technology?

< 204 >

ALSO AVAILABLE BY THE AUTHORS

Other books by Robert Weiss and Jennifer Schneider
—*Untangling the Web: Breaking Free from Sex, Porn, and Fantasy Obsession*
—*Always Turned On: Facing Sex Addiction in the Digital Age*

Other books by Robert Weiss
—*Cruise Control: Understanding Sex Addiction in Gay Men*
—*Sex Addiction 101: A Basic Guide to Healing from Sex, Porn, and Love Addiction*

Other books by Jennifer Schneider
—*Back from Betrayal: Recovering from His Affairs*
—*Disclosing Secrets: An Addict's Guide for When, to Whom, and How Much to Reveal (with Deborah Corley)*
—*Embracing Recovery from Chemical Dependency: A Personal Recovery Plan (with Deborah Corley and Richard Irons)*
—*Living with Chronic Pain: The Complete Health Guide to the Causes and Treatment of Chronic Pain*
—*Sex, Lies, and Forgiveness: Couples Speak Out on Healing from Sex Addiction (with Burt Schneider)*
—*Surviving Disclosure: A Partner's Guide for Healing the Betrayal of Intimate Trust (with Deborah Corley)*
—*The Wounded Healer: Addiction-Sensitive Approach to the Sexually Exploitative Professional (with Richard Irons)*
—*Understand Yourself, Understand Your Partner: The Essential Enneagram Guide to a Better Relationship (with Ron Corn)*

< 205 >

ABOUT THE AUTHORS

Robert Weiss LCSW, CSAT-S, is an author, clinical trainer, addiction psychotherapist and authority on the interaction of digital technology with sexual health, relationships and addiction. Currently serving as Senior Vice-President of Clinical Development for Elements Behavioral Health, Mr. Weiss has developed ongoing clinical addiction treatment programs for The Ranch in Nunnelly, TN, Promises Treatment Centers in Malibu, CA, The Sexual Recovery Institute in Los Angeles, CA (founded by Mr. Weiss in 1995) and the Life Healing Center of Santa Fe, NM. Mr. Weiss is a licensed, UCLA MSW graduate and early trainee of Dr. Patrick Carnes, an international leader in addiction treatment. He is the author of four books, numerous peer-reviewed articles, and book chapters.

Mr. Weiss has served as a media specialist in the area of sex addiction and the role of digital technology in our relationships for CNN, the Oprah Winfrey Network, the *New York Times, LA Times* and the *Today* show, *Dateline NBC* among many others. He contributes regularly to PsychCentral.com, writing primarily about sex addiction, and the Huffington Post, writing mostly about the effects of technology on communication and intimacy in relationships. Mr. Weiss has also provided clinical multi-addiction training and behavioral health program development for the National Institutes of Health, the United States military along with multiple behavioral health centers throughout the United States, Europe and Asia.

Jennifer P. Schneider, M.D., Ph.D., is a physician certified in internal medicine, addiction medicine and pain management. She is the author

< 207 >

of thirteen books, several chapters, and numerous articles in professional journals. She is a nationally recognized expert in two addiction-related fields: addictive sexual disorders and the management of chronic pain with opioids. Now retired from direct patient care, her professional activities include writing, lecturing at conferences, serving as an expert witness in legal settings, and appearing as a media guest on television and radio.

< 208 >